This is a very interesting book. It  d
social conditions in Glasgow that ith.
But it is not just about social histo
touched and changed by God an
manhood succeeded against all the odds and who has become a
leader in the Church in Scotland. A fascinating story and a book
well worth reading. I commend it to you.

Sir David McNee, K.StJ., QPM

Easy and compulsive reading, George Mitchell's autobiography
provides a fascinating slice of social history, whether of education
in Glasgow, life as a metallurgist apprentice, Bible College lecturer,
Religious Education schoolteacher or Baptist minister. It gives a
glimpse into the life of the missions that used to predominate in our
cities, and helpful insights, not least about teaching and preaching.
It refreshingly testifies to the wonderful sense of purpose and
satisfaction God gives in Jesus Christ.

Derek Prime

George Mitchell is a larger than life character. I am so glad he has
put the story of his varied life into print. It is a rattling good read
which has many lessons to teach on the way whilst providing us all
with a great testimony to God's power and grace.

Derek J. Tidball
Principal, London Bible College

George Mitchell has had an interesting and varied life. He tells the story of God's dealings with him most attractively and, as those who know him would anticipate, with many a humorous touch. He has the gift of taking us with him into some scene or to some event or into contact with some personality with just a few words, so that we cannot help visualising it all as we read. I greatly enjoyed it and could not put it down until I had read it all.

Geoffrey Grogan

Having personally 'comfae' Glasgow and starting in the Rottenrow where George Mitchell started, I found the book historically, culturally and socially excellent, doing justice to the great City of Glasgow. The book captivates the heart, demanding to be read, cover to cover. It is a book that will be appreciated by all, not only Glaswegians. Certainly a book that should be in every Glasgwegian's home. It is true in depicting what God can do in one life 'from the gutter-most to the utter-most', tracing the hand of God throughout the life of God's servant.

Bill Gilvear

'COMFY GLASGOW GAUN ELSEWHERE'

AN EXPRESSION OF THANKS

GEORGE J. MITCHELL

Kenwil Print and Design, Kirkintilloch G66 1XF

George and Jean Mitchell

ISBN 1 85792 444 4

@ George Mitchell

First published in 1999.
Re-printed in 1999, 2000 and 2003.

by

Christian Focus Publications,
Geanies House, Fearn, Ross-shire,
Scotland, IV20 ITW, Great Britain

Original Cover design by Owen Daily

Fifth revised edition by Comfy George Publishing Co. 2011.

Printed and bound in Great Britain by
Kenwil Print and Design, Kirkintilloch
www.kenwil.co.uk

Comfy Glasgow, Gaun Elsewhere.

ISBN – 13 978-0-9556964-3-5

Contents:

The title 'Comfy Glasgow' deserves some explanation. It is first of all a description of origin, where the '-fy' of' comfy' in the vernacular, signifies 'from'. I was born and bred in the 'Dear Green Place', the City of Glasgow. The title is also a description of my emotional warmth in relation to the city, which I think of like a child thinks of his friendly Mammy, in which case the comfy image indicates that I am at ease, or comfortable, thinking about Glasgow, one of the finest cities on our planet. I think Glasgow is the only city in the world with a prayer for its motto: 'Lord. Let Glasgow flourish by the preaching of the Word, and the praising of Your name.' Glasgow is one of the few cities where you can read tomorrow's news the night before! (The 'Daily Record' for the next day is on sale from about 10.30pm the previous night). Some critical person said it was the only city in the world where you were wakened up by the sound of the birds – coughing! This is unfair comment in what is now a smoke-free zone. I owe the city a huge spiritual debt, and I also want to tell you about that.

The 'Comfy Glasgow, Gaun Elsewhere' addition to the revised title indicates I have travelled a bit since the first publication of 'Comfy Glasgow' in 1999.

I hope that through reading this piece of social history, laced with personal experience, you will come to like Glasgow too, and share my other travels and activities.

I am grateful to so many people for being able to write this - especially my wife Jean, children Finlay and Janet, grandchildren Kirstin and Angus, daughter-in-law Fiona and son-in-law Billy, whose constant love and encouragement are a great help.

CHAPTER ONE

FROM ROTTENROW TO MANSION STREET

'ROTTENROW' – Imagine calling a Maternity Hospital after such an unpromising street name! The posh option for its meaning is the Gaelic, 'rat-an-righ', meaning 'street of the kings'. The not-so-posh option is that it refers to the squalid, rat (raton)-infested hovels in the centre of the medieval city of Glasgow. There are other streets of the same name in various parts of Britain…The area in which I was born achieved fame when the Glasgow Royal Maternity Hospital moved from St. Andrews Square in 1860, and developed into the world-class centre it became over a hundred years of its history at Rottenrow. One of the mind-stirring images of 'The Rottenrow' as the Glaswegians called it, is the centrepiece of the present Strathclyde University

Ma and Faither, 1955
at Willowbank, Dunkeld

development. This is George Wylie's 'Monument to Maternity', which depicts a giant nappy pin…

There is a Biblical slant to the name Rottenrow.

In a sense, we were all born in Rottenrow! - 'born in sin, shapen in iniquity' (Psalm 51:5). At any rate, the emerging shape in my case was quite unflattering - in Faither's words 'a wee skinned rabbit' -weighing four and a half pounds, and definitely out of season, born to my natural parents fifteen years after they had been told any children were an impossibility. Ma was 41 years old! The old man's words when he learned that she was pregnant are unprintable in any family publication. The four-and-a-half-pound weakling came away fine when Ma put me on Ostermilk...

My pedigree was singularly unpromising. In Glasgow, the Protestants sometimes say they hate the Catholics, but tend often to marry them. My mother was Mary Halfpenny (known of course, as Mary Ha'p'ny), who was a lapsed Roman Catholic, and my father was Jimmy, who would have called himself a Presbyterian atheist, and whose parents had come to Glasgow from the village of Old Deer in Aberdeenshire. William Mitchell had married Barbara Cruickshank, a 19-year-old domestic servant on 17 January 1896, and they moved to Glasgow, where he practised his craft as a policeman in Govanhill.

Granny Mitchell, Barbara Cruickshank, attended church only in the communion season, for what my father called 'a free bucket' (drink). Like most Glaswegian families, you can't go back more than a few generations until you meet an Irishman, and in this case Irish Roman Catholics, on my mother's side. My mother's parents were married in Clydebank RC Church.

A typical family quarrel broke out about the naming of the 'skinned rabbit'. Granny Mitchell had vetoed the parental choice of Willie, ruling it 'bad luck'. Grandfather Mitchell had been Willie, and he and his twenty-year-old son Leslie had died within the same week at the height of the infamous Glasgow 'flu epidemic (January 1928). So George the new baby had to be, which seemed equally bad luck, since Uncle Geordie (father Jimmy's brother) was, without going into too much unsavoury detail, the black sheep of the family.

The white ewe of the family was undoubtedly Auntie Nellie, known as 'the Hallelujah', an enthusiastic member of the Salvation Army. There was a family feeling that the split-new wean had to be 'done', so Auntie Nellie secured the services of the Possilpark Corps (Killearn Street) officer, to come to the house and 'do the needful' for wee George, under the Blood and Fire flag. The family view was that the dedication service was a bit of a flop, since the Corps officer persistently refused the 'bowlie' proffered by Granny, whose Church of Scotland pedigree made her feel that the service was incomplete without some moisturising for the wean.

Faither, 1914-18 War

Things had been very difficult before I was born. In December 1937, my mother disappeared from home, because she was so deeply in debt that she thought her husband, Jimmy, who had beaten her many times, would kill her when he found out she had to go to the debtors' court. The sad consequence of this was that he had to give up the Glasgow Corporation slum-clearance flat they had in Eagle Street, move in with Granny in Mansion Street, Possilpark, enlist the help of his family, and spend weekends hunting for his Mary. He eventually brought her home from Dundee, and reached an agreement with the courts to pay off her debts. Therefore, for the first three years of my life, I lived with Granny in Mansion Street, in the Possilpark district of Glasgow.

Hitler's insatiable appetite for lebensraum ('living-space') continued unchecked, until even the appeasers' patience ran out. World War II was declared, and Mansion Street prepared for the onslaught of Hitler's bombs.

'Mansion Street' -now there was one of the most cynical misnomers of history, quite inappropriate to describe its smoke-blackened tenements! The mansion to which it referred was probably Possil House, built around 1700, and extended by Alexander Campbell, one of Glasgow's West Indies merchants. It became the home of Sir Archibald Alison, Sheriff of Lanarkshire and distinguished historian. After his death, Walter MacFarlane bought the entire estate (105 acres in 1869), and developed fourteen acres of it into Saracen Foundry. The ornamental iron foundry had taken its name, Saracen Foundry, from the ancient and famous Glasgow pub 'The Saracen's Head' in Gallowgate, via Washington Street, and from 1872 all the work was centred on Possilpark. The work-force had grown from 120 in 1861 to around 1200 by the 1890s. It would probably sound funny for today's residents to hear that Possilpark was designed as a showpiece model suburb, with a population of over 10,000 by the 1890s. The foundry made rainwater pipes, gutters, baths, street lamps, verandahs, bandstands, fountains, and other ornamental ironwork. At the height of its fame, the foundry had a 250-page catalogue of ornamental castings which went all over the world. The designer of the works, J Boucher, included a palatial showroom area. During the two World Wars, the work was diverted to more lucrative, munitions-related products. The landscape in the Possil House estate had been systematically raped when almost all the trees in the 100-acre site were felled in the 1870s.

Mansion Street intersected Saracen Street near the Saracen Foundry, but by the time of my birth in April 1939, the tenements were smoke-blackened and grubby, and towards the Balmore Road end the tenants in the newer houses had to live down the whispered, if inaccurate, slur of being 'slum clearance'. At the pavement's edge, outside each tenement close during wartime, baffle walls were built to limit the blast during bombing, and in the absence of air-raid shelters, the residents were to gather in the back close, behind the stairs until the All Clear sounded.

My memories of this period are the fleeting images of childhood. Firstly, there was the regular 'hing' (hang) alongside Granny, who would put a cushion on their first floor front room window-sill, and lean out of the window to watch the customers going into Mr Birrell's grocery shop underneath, and the other shops around. Then there were tramcars galore to be seen and heard rattling along Saracen Street, many of them heading for the haven of Possilpark depot nearby, air brakes whistling as they turned the corner into the now hawthorn-less Hawthorn Street. There was the occasional excitement of some special consignment of castings leaving from Saracen Foundry in Hawthorn Street.

The back-court excitement consisted of loud family quarrels from time to time, usually about whose turn it was to wash the stairs in the tenement, or the state of the stair-head lavatories, We also had the occasional noise of the plaintive singing of a tramp popularly known as 'Johnny Hunnercoats' (the human onion), doing renditions of 'O Sole Mio', which were shouted down, and sometimes money was thrown in exchange for a quick move to a more distant audience.

I had vague memories of being taken down to the close until the 'All Clear' was sounded after a German air attack. Mansion Street was protected from the blast of air raids by having baffle walls built opposite each close, at the edge of the pavement. I remember walking into one of these baffle walls, which gave me a pain in the head. As President Reagan is supposed to have said when he phoned the Pope after he got shot (according to a Glasgow joke) 'It's sore, I'n'tit?' ie getting shot, or in my case, walking into a baffle wall. My head was sore for days.

I remember being taken for walks out and about with Ma and Granny, as a toddler and as a wee boy. On one occasion, I had to go to the public lavatory when I was out with Granny. I emerged clutching a ten-shilling note I had found. From then on, whenever I was out with Granny, I was sent into the public lavatory, just in case...

The space problems in Granny's Mansion Street apartment were not helped by the need to accommodate my mother, father, me, my big brother Jim, my Granny, and her lodger Bobby. (I have often tried to figure out what the sleeping arrangements were). The family had thought of the stay at Granny's as only a temporary measure. Imagine the delight when a school friend of Faither offered the family the tenancy of a cottage at his smallholding in Lambhill, at a nominal rental, in exchange for feeding his pigs at weekends! They moved there when I was three, shortly before my brother Jim struck fear in the German war machine by volunteering, on his eighteenth birthday, to join His Majesty's wartime forces.

CHAPTER TWO
MEET THE FAMILY

I suppose it is time to introduce you in more detail to my family – Faither Jimmy, Ma Mary, and my big brother Jim.

Faither was a striking figure about six feet tall, and about fifteen stones in weight. He had hugely muscled forearms, and massive biceps, rather like Popeye the Sailor Man, one arm suitably tattooed. He was the epitome of the 'horny-handed sons of toil'. The palms and insides of the fingers of his huge hands were covered with a horn-like hard material, which fissured into hacks in winter. One of my memories, (I can almost smell it as I write this), was of my father sitting stooped over the fire, rubbing a strong-smelling, yellowy-green coloured compound called 'Snowfire' into his hacks, before going out to his work (constant nightshift). The ends of his thick, nicotine-stained fingers were protected by black broken fingernails, like Billy Bones in 'Treasure Island'. He always took with him his tin 'piece-box', which was shaped like a slice of plain bread. We did not have the same bewildering options in buying bread as today, and the plain loaf, with a curved dark top, and a lighter, straight foot, was the fare of the working classes. A pan loaf was more square in section, with pale crusts, and anyone with upwardly mobile desires or speech patterns was said in Glasgow to be 'pan loaf'. Faither also carried his oval, mini-keg-shaped tea and sugar box, with the tea and sugar stamp in each half.

Faither was 16 when World War II broke out in 1914. He was called up into the Army, and fought against the 'savage Hun' (the Germans) in France, and against 'Johnny Turk' in Mesopotamia. I can remember only two stories he told me about the War. The first was about a cook who stepped out of the field kitchen to open a tin of bully beef, and was shot at by a sniper. The bullet went through the tin into the cook's arm, and he said they were picking bits of bully beef out of his arm… When Faither was wounded in Mesopotamia, Granny Mitchell sent him a parcel containing a cake and a pair of socks. By the time the parcel reached him, the mould from the cake was growing through the socks.

Faither's total share of the spoils of war consisted of a bayonet, and a German Army belt with 'Gott Mit Uns' on the buckle. Amid the massive carnage of the conflict, the German propaganda, like the British, taught them that God was on their side.

Faither's other legacy of the War was a few songs they sang in the trenches. He taught me songs like 'Pack up your troubles in your old kit bag', 'It's a long way to Tipperary', a romantic song 'Roses of Picardy', and 'Mademoiselle from Armentieres':

'Mademoiselle from Armentieres, Parley Voo,
Mademoiselle from Armentieres, Parley Voo
Mademoiselle from Armentieres,
She hasn't been kissed for forty years,
Inky Pinky Parley Voo...'

Mademoiselle from Armentieres, Parley Voo,
Mademoiselle from Armentieres, Parley Voo
You might forget the gas and shell,
You'll never forget the Mademoiselle,
Inky Pinky Parley Voo.'

This song was sung by the French Army in the 1830s, and during the Franco-Prussian War of 1870s, and was picked up in 1914 by the 'Old Contemptibles' of the British Army. They supposedly chose this nickname in response to Kaiser Wilhelm II's scathing dismissal of the 1914 British forces as 'a contemptible little army.'

Back to the main plot!
I remembered Faither as bald-headed. He always wore a worker's cap, at a jaunty angle. He bought his caps from Hoey's in Springburn, but if he could afford it at the time, he went to Dunn the Gents' Outfitter in Sauchiehall Street. He got his suits from either the Fifty Shilling Tailor, or the Thirty Shilling Tailor. I remember the shop in the arcade at Stow Street, off Cowcaddens.

At weekends he liked to dress up for going to football at Keppoch Park, home of Glasgow Perthshire, a Junior League football team, and after teatime he spent Saturday evenings in Mallan's Pub in Kilfinan Street, Lambhill. He always wore boots, because he had a weakened ankle after falling from a stool he was standing on while wall-papering a room. He referred to his working boots as 'tackety boots', and his weekend, soft-leather boots as 'sparables', because of the headless nails used to fasten the soles and heels...

After a period spent working with a lemonade firm, Faither joined the Glasgow Corporation Tramways Department (Permanent Way) in 1930, driving the works car, and functioning as a rail-fitter and burner, repairing track throughout the night. As a measure of his physical strength, where others wheeled their steel cylinders of oxygen/acetylene in a wheelbarrow, Faither often carried his on his shoulder.

He was not keen on bullies. Many years later, his ex-workmates gave me a glimpse of the calibre of the man when they told me how he cured a bully of his bullying. Faither had seen a small work-mate in the Sawmillfield Street depot being bullied. One night, Faither was teamed up with the bully, and inverted a dustbin over him in a back court, pinning his arms to his side, and then beat him round a backcourt with a number ten shovel. This seemed to them a good Jimmy Mitchell Cure for bullying.

Faither was very clever practically, building things, and mending things, sawing logs for the winter fires and stacking them at the end of the cottage. He gave the cottage a treatment of Irish lime each spring, and kept a well-stocked garden, with good fruit and veg. We had plum trees, blackcurrant bushes, and a gooseberry bush. He grew cabbages and cauliflower, onions, leeks and potatoes (Kerrs pinks and golden wonders), lettuces and parsley. He liked flowers, and grew dahlias, gladioli, chrysanthemums and marigolds.

One year we had a bumper harvest of pail-full after pail-full of plums. All of this was a paradise in play opportunities for a small boy who had seen only the grimy tenements of Possilpark.

Faither always wrote with a Swan fountain pen, which was his pride and joy. The only remaining specimens I have of his lovely handwriting are his signature on my school report card, and his careful copy of our dog's pedigree! He filled in his Littlewoods football pools form every week with his pen. We had a ceramic tobacco jar in the shape of a pig on the mantelpiece. Faither used to give his pools coupon a ritual rub on a ceramic pig's nose each week, hoping for luck when he posted it! As far as I know, he never won anything on the pools.

Faither loved jokes and Scottish songs. Although we suffered because of his appetite for booze, I have to admit that drink softened his nature. He loved the country life in Lambhill, and read the 'Scottish Farmer' every week. He enjoyed his involvement with animals, especially his beloved pigs.

He tried to improve our conditions, and when I was about nine years old he bought a Cossar battery accumulator radio to conquer the problem of not having electricity. We always had one battery on the radio, and one on charge in David Hope's electrical shop in Saracen Street, Possilpark.

Faither was a hard worker, and in many ways a tough guy. He never told me that he loved me (he would have reckoned that was soft) but he proved his love in many ways by doing many loving things for me. He built me a super swing with chains prepared by the blacksmith at his work. He built a luxury, free-standing rabbit hutch, and bought me a big rabbit, which we christened 'Percy' for some unknown reason. He built a 'doocot' (dove-cote, ie pigeon-house), and installed some white fantail pigeons in it for my amusement. He occasionally took us to the Metropole Theatre in the city, and on public holidays when he was off work we went down the Clyde from the Broomielaw on the Queen Mary II, or to Helensburgh on the train. On the boat, he used to go, so he told me, to inspect the engines, but was really at the bar. When we went 'doon the watter', he used to satisfy his grisly sense of humour by taking a couple of rolls liberally spread with mustard,

Gran Maclean at Lambhill Post Office
1958

and he threw pieces to the seagulls and waited for the fun. We had an occasional visit to the Metropole Theatre to see the Logan Family. His normal euphemism for visiting Mallan's pub every Saturday was that he was going to the optician to 'see about his glasses'. I found out later what that really meant. One Saturday night, he came home from the pub drunk, and insisted on going out to feed the rabbit. When we went out some time later to see what had happened to him he was standing, fast asleep, leaning on the top of the rabbit hutch.

He had an almost pastoral interest in the pigs, and one Saturday night, he missed his normal activities to go chasing after a runaway pig he called 'the hurdle-jumper'. This pig seemed to be able to escape from any pigsty, and head for the open country in the area of the cottage. That was the evening I learned for the first time the past tense of a certain verb. He captured the pig, but came home confessing to Ma that he had 'shat himself' in the heat of the chase.

In the final weeks of our stay at Lochside Cottage, he had to sell our nanny goat as there would be no room for her in a Possilpark tenement flat. Two boys from Maryhill answered the advert, and asked him solemnly whether the goat was pedigreed. He told them that the goat had a better pedigree than them! They bought Nanny, and went on their way rejoicing.

I saw Faither crying occasionally at Hogmanay, and only on one other occasion. When all the pigs had to be slaughtered because of an outbreak of swine fever, I was warned not to come near, or look into the boiler-house. I looked in, and saw him in blood-soaked oilskins, with a pig-sticking knife, crying like a baby because he had to kill his beloved pigs.

Faither always showed an interest in my progress at school, and often kept out of bed after his Friday nightshift to watch me playing for Possil Primary School football team on Saturday mornings. He watched from a distance, probably because he couldn't face the prospect of talking to my teacher on the sidelines. He sometimes told me I had played 'no bad', which made me glow with pleasure.

He had been through the Depression, so he would never touch booze through the week, in case he lost his job. He seemed always to be trying to make up for it at weekends, and the family budget suffered severely as a result.

What about Mother Mary, or Molly, as Faither called her in his softer moments? I called her 'Ma'. She was a kind, gentle generous and harmless lady, with a loving, outgoing nature. She had been brought up in Lambhill by her granny. During the First World War, she worked on munitions at Lochburn Foundry, the ruins of which could be seen in my childhood near the West Highland (railway) Line, and the pedestrian tunnel called 'The Hallowe'en Pend' under the Forth and Clyde canal. This tunnel was sometimes used by courting couples, and enabled folk to go from Lochburn Road to Hillend Road, or over the hill to Ruchill Golf Course.

When she was a young person, Ma used to go dancing to the Hibs (Hibernian) Hall, just across the Lambhill canal bridge on Balmore Road. The Hibs Hall was originally known as 'The Stables', because it was a staging post for exchanging the draught horses which pulled barges along the canal. The barges conveyed freight in the early half of the nineteenth century, before railways came into prominence. In my childhood, the Stables was a depot for storing chemicals used by Alex Thom the coal firm, who also did some haulage work, carrying drums of chemicals from Cooper, MacDougall and Robertson's works in Lochburn Road.

The Lambhill Stables Project has transformed the old building, and it has been wonderfully refurbished, and there are great plans for its future use in the community of Lambhill, and my Ma danced in it! Ma loved coming back to live in her beloved Lambhill. She looked after her hens like a mother hen, and enjoyed baking and entertaining visitors. She was generally short of cash, but was very kind with what she had. When they lived in Eagle Street, a slum clearance area off Craighall Road, she always gave a neighbour's son a shilling on a Friday morning, to buy rolls for his family. The neighbour returned it every Friday evening when they got their wages (I heard this from the neighbour's son).

Ma called Thursday 'the day before tomorrow', because Faither came off the nightshift with his pay on Friday mornings. Ma was under pressure to provide ten of Faither's minimum of twenty cigarettes a day. He went into a bad mood if she bought the Co-op brand of cigarettes, Shipmate and Cogent. She did this occasionally and paid for them on Fridays. Faither was a 'Capstan Full Strength' smoker, but as time went on he moved to 'Senior Service' and later to 'Piccadilly Number One', a very mild cigarette, possibly because his throat was bothering him.

Ma's way of buying clothes and extras was to buy Provident or Caledonian cheques. Even as a child I detected the nuances of sales staff when they asked Ma, 'How are you paying?' They had a different scale of prices for those who had 'Provvie cheques', which seemed unjust.. Ma seemed always to be in debt, and always paying off collectors. She was not good at managing money. We used the facilities of the pawnshop regularly. It is interesting to note that pawnshops have made a comeback in recent years. Their interest rates were astronomical when you thought of them long-term, but they were good for immediate cash, short-term, for the poor. There were two pawnshops in Possilpark: McManus' at the Balmore Road/Bardowie Street corner, and Quigley's in Barloch Street. I also seem to remember a pawnshop called Christies, off the Garscube Road, near Lyon Street and Raglan Street. Their advert, painted on the corner of the building, read: 'Are you like the baker, needing dough? We lend money, don't you know!' I used to hide the brown paper parcel containing Faither's good suit in my schoolbag, and run in to Possilpark after school. The pawnbroker's assistant would give me money and a pawn ticket which I had to guard with my life. It was instant cash on a Thursday, but the suit had to be redeemed on a Friday so that the old man would be able to be dressed for attending his football match and going to the pub on Saturdays.

Ma's other escape routes from being skint were Nicholson's the metal merchant off Saracen Street in Possilpark, who would give a few shillings for a piece of lead or copper, or she could take rags to the Briggate down by the River Clyde.

The only time Ma had money was when Faither died (August 1956), and she got his insurance money. Unfortunately her pals were in need – a Sofona fireplace here, a new bed or chair somewhere else, and the money soon vanished. When Ma died in 1971, I found her little notebook with its record of what had been loaned and what had been returned, and threw it in the fire.

People liked Ma, and she had some loyal friends. One of them used to help her out, and I was sent to return money that had been borrowed. When I had chickenpox, she asked another friend to lend some books, and I enjoyed reading them and wished we had some more. The only book in the house originally was 'Uncle Tom's Cabin by Harriet Beecher Stowe. I read with horror about the treatment of slaves in America's Deep South. It is amazing, in the providence of God, that I have found great joy in helping and teaching Africans. Later, when Ma was skint again, she asked a friend for a pair of her daughter's old gym knickers so that I could learn to swim! She couldn't afford to buy me swimming trunks. That is how I became an early cross-dresser!

One episode in my childhood revealed another example of the kind of lady Ma was. One Saturday evening we were walking around enjoying the sunshine, when we heard a noise in one of the outhouses. We discovered a young woman and her two little girls cowering in the shed. They were squatters. Ma listened to their story, and persuaded Faither to take them into the cottage to stay with us. She got a Provident cheque, and bought them all new clothes and shoes. The Mother was rigged out in what was called 'The New Look.' Ma was paying off that stuff for months on end. They lived in the big room, where we had a bed settee. Unfortunately, the Mother got too friendly with a lorry driver, and became pregnant. Her baby was born on our settee, and it was of course ruined and had to be flung out. Faither's objections were final, and arrangements were made (I knew nothing about that) so that the family could move out after being with us for more than a year. We never heard from them again.

In later life I have reflected on that episode. Many people would have dismissed Ma as a mug, and her action as stupidity. I think she was a kind person reacting to a need. To love is to be vulnerable. I have spent a lot of time in the company of Christian people, and I cannot think of many who would be able to match her level of generosity.

I have to confess my part in Ma's physical condition. She was told she couldn't have children, but fifteen years after they had adopted my big brother Jim, when Ma was 41 years old, she became pregnant! Her blood pressure caused concern, and she was in hospital for the later stages, but on Easter Monday 1939, I was born, as one out of due time, the natural son of both parents!

There were one or two spin-offs from my birth. Faither stopped being physically violent to Ma.

Secondly, Ma's health was possibly affected. She was troubled by high blood pressure for a good part of her life. She would occasionally take terrible nose bleeds, when basins would be needed, and great gouts of blood would be lost. In 1955, when I was taking my Scottish Higher exams, what was called the 'report line' of her serious illness went out three times from Stobhill Hospital. She recovered, and a new doctor came to our practice. He took a great interest in her, and found a drug which gave relief. She lived until 1971.

What about big brother Jim? Faither was not wholly in agreement with his adoption, but screening processes were not so severe in those days. Faither was not very interested in Jim, and was disappointed that he was a slow learner and needed help in his schooling. Jim volunteered for the Army on his eighteenth birthday in November 1942. This act transformed the relationship between Jim and Faither! Jim had proved his manhood! In September 1944, as part of the clearing-up operation before the paratroopers were dropped at Arnheim, Jim's unit was sent in. 'Operation Market Garden' was a fiasco. Patton never approved of it, Eisenhower endorsed it reluctantly, and Churchill saw the dangers, although he saw it as a possible way of speeding the end of the War. The German forces were much stronger than the Allies thought. Jim's unit was surrounded by a Hitler Youth battalion. He was taken by troop train to Czechoslovakia as a prisoner-of-war. They were hungry in the Stalag. Jim told me their best meal was when they killed and ate an Alsatian guard dog. After a few months, Jim escaped.

He and the other prisoners were marched each day across a bridge and through a village, and were made to cut pit props in a nearby wood for the Nazi war effort . Jim dodged under a bridge one day, and stood in the water chest-deep until darkness fell. He always had a good sense of direction, and headed west. He travelled by night, and hid in haylofts and woods through the day. He was picked up by the advancing American forces, and passed through the lines. That was how he made his way from Czechoslovakia to Lochside Cottage Lambhill. He was so thin, the dog didn't even recognise him.

After his demob in May 1947, he was not happy in Civvy Street, and rejoined the Army on a twelve-year engagement in September 1947. He served with the Seaforth Highlanders in Malaya from 1947 until 1950, and saw action in the wild period before General Templar took command and sorted out the snipers. After Malaya, he was transferred into the Glasgow Regiment, The Highland Light Infantry, which he hated. He volunteered for the Korean War to get out of the HLI! He fought with the Kosbies (Kings Own Scottish Borderers) in the Korean War(1950-53). He was a bren-gunner, and took part in 'Charlie Chinaman's Gunpowder Plot', a Chinese offensive on 4-5 November , when Bill Speakman, a member of Jim's 'C' Company, won a Victoria Cross in the action. Jim was wounded, and had to go to Japan for skin grafts on his legs, which were burned when a shell hit a petrol can near him, and it exploded. Jim also served in Aden, and Gibraltar (as a snooker room attendant!), and Germany. When Jim was in Malaya, he was a five-star private, but he was upset because they were going to reduce his wages because he did not have a Third Class Education Certificate. I felt it was my duty as the kid brother to teach him how to do fractions, decimals, and percentages. Imagine my joy when he wrote me the only letter I ever received from him, to tell me that he'd passed his Third Class Education Certificate. I still have it in the tin box with his medals and service record.

There was great rejoicing when Jim came home on leave. He used to bring home duty-free cigarettes, so that Faither could smoke his head off for weeks on end. He used to buy all the comics, which he and I read – the Adventure, Wizard, Hotspur and Rover every week. I made the acquaintance of Roy of the Rovers, Alf Tupper (the Tough of the Track who trained on fish suppers), Wilson who ran up Mount Everest in his black combinations, Deliberate Daniel the thinking man's gunslinger, and sundry other comic-book heroes. Jim was also able to enjoy Ma's home cooking. She made very good scones, especially soda scones, and pancakes.

Faither died of cancer of the throat in August 1956, after a short illness. He was moved from Oakbank Hospital in Baird's Brae to Ruchill Hospital in Bilsland Drive. The first sign of serious illness was his loss of speech. He spent the last six weeks of his life writing messages to us on a Basildon Bond writing-pad Ma had bought. Jim gave up the Army on completion of his twelve-year engagement, and came home. He was there to look after Ma, and I was free to go to London to study, in 1960.

After Ma's death in 1971, I looked after Jim.

CHAPTER THREE

THE DEAD CENTRE OF GLASGOW

We moved from Mansion Street, Possilpark, to Lochside Cottage, Lambhill, in 1942, when I was three years old.

Lambhill! The very name conjured up bucolic images of grassy slopes with innocent, woolly creatures and new vistas! There were grassy slopes and good expanses of water, and many trees in the area – a child's paradise! There were also about eighty coal pits, a few iron foundries, and steel constructors, and the Forth and Clyde canal, with its busy banks, flowing through the village.

Lambhill was one of the peripheral villages on the north of Glasgow which succumbed to the spreading tentacles of the extending city, and by so doing, contributed to Glasgow's variety and character. Just as the American West was opened up by the railroad pushing west, so in Glasgow, in a kind of comic parallel, it was the spread of the tramcar routes which signalled the end of the independent existence of villages like Lambhill, Partick, and Maryhill. Comic, because the Glasgow equivalent to America's snorting locomotive monster was the slow-moving, clanking tramcar, rattling over its rails and points, like an iron granny with her corsets creaking. The end of the line at Lambhill terminus was reached by a right-angle left turn into Strachur Street (formerly Drummond Street and Drummond's Land).

There were no formal boundaries to Lambhill, but the consensus was that it started at Possil Station in Balmore Road and finished at Blackhill Cottages, a miners' row beyond Lambhill Cemetery. Its east-west boundaries were the cluster of houses along the banks of the Forth and Clyde Canal at the Shangie, and the bridge over the West Highland (Glasgow to Fort William) railway line, short of Cooper, MacDougall and Robertson's Chemical Works. The tram terminus was an important reference point, as was the main bridge over the Forth and Clyde Canal on Balmore Road. The old wooden lifting bridge across the canal was replaced by a modem bascule (from the French 'seesaw') bridge in 1934.

Lochside Cottage

The cottage was built in the early 1700s. If you crossed the bridge, and turned immediately left along the canal bank, it was located down a dip about half a mile from the Lambhill Canal Bridge, beside West Possil Loch, which gradually disappeared throughout my ten years there, as the lorries tipped their loads on what was called the coup beside it. A family of swans lived on a little island in the centre of the Loch. We moved there because we got the cottage for a peppercorn rent, in exchange for Faither feeding his pal's pigs each weekend.. The smallholding was called 'Graham's Piggery', and the nearest neighbours lived in Lochend House nearby. Jock Munro was a blaes, sand and gravel merchant who lived there with his family.

Lochside cottage was a whitewashed, up-and-downstairs affair with a living room with a fire and range, including an oven, and a sink by the window. There was a step down into the front room, which toffs would have called the parlour, which had an open fire, two bedrooms, and a small bedroom which was really as small as a box-room. The 1849 census listed 15 people living there, including a farmer and two ploughmen and their families. I used to wonder about the sleeping arrangements in those far-off days.

There was no gas, no electricity, no inside toilet, no bath. Sometimes at weekends we had log or coal fires in the big room, when other relatives came for the monthly card school. They played rummy for small stakes. When it became dark, it was a bit like the cowboy movies, as we lit the wicks on our paraffin lamps. Later on when things got modernised, we had Tilley and Colman lamps, fuelled with paraffin, with silk tie-on mantles. These later lamps were preheated with a fibre clip soaked in methylated spirits, and the unpardonable sin was to bump the frail mantle…

There was deep joy when Faither brought home a battery accumulator radio, and we could listen to Paul Temple and Dick Barton, Donald Peers, and the Palm Court Orchestra with Max Jaffa, Chapel in the Valley, and The Man in Black(Valentine Dyall). Sometimes the power gave out (usually on a Monday, in the middle of Dick Barton, Special Agent!), and there was no radio until after school on Tuesday when I went in to David Hope's electrical shop in Saracen Street to leave the spent battery and collect the re-charged one. We forget, in our fully carpeted and centrally heated homes now, what it was like to live where there was usually only one source of heat in the house, and in our case, one rug in the living room and linoleum (Ma called it 'wax-cloth') as the floor covering, except when we stepped down into the sitting room, and the linoleum was laid out in squares. Most Sunday nights, we used the sitting room, and had a log fire, and luxuriated.

Our gramophone was a wind-up contraption, which used steel gramophone needles, and I remember our first records were: 'Open the door, Richard', Al Jolson's 'Rock-a-bye Your Baby to a Dixie Melody', and 'The Shilling a Week Man'.

As well as the trees, grass and water around the place, there were four outhouses, two with earth floors, and a wrecked bread-van which served in a wide variety of dramatic roles -stagecoach, ship and tank - as small boys played out their cinematic fantasies. We built huts up trees, and got into trouble with Faither for using the nails from his tool-box. We also used one of the outhouses as the venue for a child card school.

The cottage was conveniently near the canal, and in the summer we had great fun, paddling, swimming and fishing. Near the Shangie there was an expanse of water in the Possil Loch, a seventy-acre bird sanctuary, but it was only useful to me and my pals for the bulrushes and bird-nesting. The most modest area of water in Lambhill lay between Knapdale Street and Balmore Road, behind Thom's Coalyard, and was called 'The Pudge'. Much rafting was done there, using discarded oil and chemical drums lashed to wood with baling rope.

Across the corner of the field on the south-west of the Cottage, was a swampy area thick with frogspawn in spring, and 'baggie minnows' and dragonflies in summer, leading into Lochside Loch. I found the remains of an old skater's chair, and old skating boots. Sometimes I used to lean on the fence looking out to the loch, and try to visualise the special trains my father had told me about, running out from town on winter evenings, the crowds of excited skaters and sledge chairs whizzing on the ice, skating at night on a loch illuminated by naphtha lamps, enjoying teas and refreshments from stalls conveniently situated. The loch which gave Lochside its name was still good for rafting during my boyhood, although we had to be careful to avoid the swan's nest on a small island in the middle of the loch, especially as the area of water diminished each year before the advancing coup with its sulphurous smells.

There was the greatest possible contrast between the idylls of play and the grim realities of day-to-day living.

The Castle

The most imposing building in the area was Lambhill House, or 'The Castle', as it was known locally. Its origins went back to the Hutchesons and the Grahams. Thomas Hutcheson of Lambhill was born about 1520 and died around 1594. His eldest son was George, who was born between 1550 and 1560, probably 1558, and died in December 1639. The youngest son was Thomas, who was born in 1589 and died on 1st September 1641, aged 52. He conveyed to the Corporation of Glasgow certain heritable subjects so that a hospital could be built, and endowed 20,000 merks (around £ 1, 1 00 sterling) for a school for educating and harbouring twelve boys, 'indigent orphans', who would be 'maintained in the Hospital with meat, drink, clothes, elding (fuel) and other necessities as becomes...' Thus the Hutcheson Hospital, Hutcheson's Grammar School, and the Hutcheson Foundation began. George Hutcheson purchased the lands of Over and Nether Gairbraid in 1600. The Gairbraid Estate passed to their nephew Ninian Hill, and eventually to Mary Hill, after whom the district was named. In 1763, Mary Hill, the Gairbraid heiress, married Robert Graham, who had at some point in his career been captured and enslaved by Algerian pirates. Robert's fortune was secure when the Forth and Clyde Canal was taken through the Gairbraid Estate, and its northern area was laid out in feus for an industrial village. Robert Graham died in 1804, and Mary in 1809, and both are buried in the grounds of Glasgow Cathedral. There is a 1788 sketch of Lambhill House, by William Graham, whose family lived there until the early twentieth century. It was taken over by Glasgow Corporation, who turned it into homes for working-class families, mainly miners, who had been evicted from colliery-owned homes during a strike.

In our time, as boys and girls, we spent many happy hours playing in its grounds, and in the adjoining field, which belonged to a farmer called Stein, whose farmhouse was in Lochburn Road. The grass in front of the Castle was a drying green, and the residents used to beat their carpets there.

The front gate of the place was technically known as 791 Balmore Road, and the families living there in my time were the Andersons, the Browns, the Freedmans, Catherine Gregory, the McLeans, Annie Marshall, Alex ('Sanny') Munro and his wife Annie, the Scotts, the Smiths, and the Middletons in a neat house behind the main one, and a colourful son James, who came home on leave wearing a splendid Scots Guards uniform. The main building had a wash-house with a careful rota of users. For a time, the Castle grounds had a gypsy caravan behind the main building. This fascinated us as boys, and we just had to break into it, and see the dark secrets of the fortune-tellers.

When V.E. Day (Victory in Europe) day occurred, we marked the occasion with a huge bonfire in the Castle grounds, on 8 May 1945, with great rejoicing, potatoes taken from Mr Stein's field and roasted in the bonfire, and the effigy of Adolf Schickelgruber (Hitler) burning away merrily!

The Cemeteries

The Castle was bounded along the edge of Balmore Road by a very high wall, and on Sundays the pavement was thronged with people, given decent weather, making their way out to the cemetery.

The crowds passed Nellie the flower seller, who was succeeded by Annie Munro, who sold flowers from a little wooden hut at the Castle gate.

Although Lambhill is in the north of the city, it is known as 'the dead centre of Glasgow' because it has a Protestant Cemetery, a Catholic Cemetery (St Kentigern's), a Jewish Cemetery, and, in case you thought you'd escaped, Glasgow Crematorium, with its neighbouring burial ground, the Western Necropolis, which is, strictly speaking, in Maryhill. The (Greek) title Necropolis ('death city') is shared with its more illustrious neighbour near Glasgow Cathedral, and typifies the Victorian interest in death.

The Scottish War Graves Commission have taken care to recognise the final sacrifice made in War. The Cross of Sacrifice beside the crematorium has a screen wall behind it bearing the names of Scottish regiments, many of whom had their headquarters in Glasgow during both wars, notably the Glasgow Regiment, the Highland Light Infantry. The Boer War memorial stands opposite the Cross of Sacrifice.

There is a large stone commemorating the Cadder Pit Disaster of Sunday 3rd August 1913, when twenty-two miners died in a fire disaster in the nearby Carron Company's Number 15 Cadder Pit, at the edge of Cadder Woods. The shaft was 169 fathoms deep, and fire broke out in a cabin near the bottom of the shaft about 4.30 pm. By 7.30 pm there were twenty-two deaths, twelve widows, and forty-one fatherless children. The disaster aroused tremendous emotion and sympathy throughout Scotland. We could also see the grave of Benny Lynch, the Glasgow kid who made it as world champion boxer at bantamweight, and Will Fyffe, the Scottish comedian who wrote 'I belong to Glasgow'.

The Scottish Burial Reform and Cremation Society was founded in August 1888 by two doctors, a sanitary engineer, and an architect. Sir John Mann, a distinguished Chartered Accountant in Glasgow, was the first Secretary of the Society. In the early days, a visitor, Keir Hardie, the founder of the Independent Labour Party handed in 'a crumpled 20 shilling Scottish bank note', and became a shareholder. The crematorium was opened in 1895, the oldest in Scotland, and the third oldest in the UK. The first cremation was carried out on 13 April 1895.

The crematorium was designed in the Gothic Revival style, and includes very rare marble in the shafts of the pillars.

Keir Hardie was cremated there on 29 September, 1915, so you could say of Keir Hardie that he did not only put his money where his mouth was; he also put his body where his fire was......

We'll say more about death, burial and cremation later.

Each Sunday in the summer months, a local character called 'Blind Mary' would walk out from the tram terminus, wearing voluminous clothing including as the outer layer an oilskin gas cape, carrying a stool and a Braille Bible. She used to sit with her back to the highest section of the Castle wall, and read her Braille Bible, with an enamel mug on a string, hoping for help from the passing throng. The activities of the wee Lambhill boys, who were not averse to walking in file and dropping stones into her begging mug, or dropping 'sticky wullies' on to her hair from a great height above the Castle wall, led her to use some loud, and definitely un-Biblical, language.

The Canal

The Forth and Clyde Canal which was crossed in Balmore Road by the modem bascule bridge, was built as a result of the canal mania which gripped Britain in the 1760s. Work began on l0th June 1768, and it had reached Hamilton Hill in Glasgow before the cash which had funded the project ran out. Confiscated Jacobite money from forfeited estates enabled the job to be completed to the Clyde in 1790. Then the work was extended to the new village of Port Dundas (named in honour later of Lord Dundas, governor of the Canal Company), in 1790. The Canal was managed by the Caledonian

Railway from 1867 until 1948, when it was taken over by the British Transport Commission, and passed to the British Waterways Board in 1962. I was of course oblivious to all this, and thought of the canal as a good place to swim and fish, its banks as a good place for sun-bathing, and an event-full place replete with lore, some of which I had experienced first hand. There was the evening a horse was grazing while its cart was being unloaded, and it was driven down the slope by the weight of the cart, and drowned at Larnbhill Bridge. Then I was there when they fished out the bloated body of a woman, again near the Lambhill Bridge, which was the stuff of nightmares for some of the lads who witnessed it. The Stables project includes some exciting ideas to extend public use of and interest in the canal. Mr Gordon Turner lived in a cottage beside the old stables building. He was the canal banksman, who was born into a canal working family who lived in a cottage at Stockingfield, Maryhill. Mrs Margaret Sexton, Mr Turner's daughter, recently described how the family left by barge in 1954 to take the canal cottage at Firhill. Mr Turner's dishevelled appearance because of his work earned him the nickname 'Lana' by ironic contrast with the glamorous film-star of the period, Lana Turner

Lambhill Iron Works
Going towards the city, Lambhill Iron Works spread along the area on the city side of the canal bank, to the right, at the end of Strachur Street. The main gate was straight ahead of the end of the tram rails in the terminus.

The Company was launched in the 1850s as Robert Laidlaw and Sons, gas and water engineers. Its main product was structural steelwork for the building industry. It occupied the site of the former Lambhill Foundry and Lambhill Forge, which had produced crank and propellor shafts for the Clyde's burgeoning shipbuilding industry. The Iron Works produced bomb casings during the First World War. By our time, the works supplied structural steelwork mainly for the building industry.

Many good craftsmen were trained there, and went on to higher things. A Lambhill man, William Gillies of Lambhill Mission, worked as a draughtsman at Lambhill Iron Works, and left to work with Colvilles Ltd. in the Lanarkshire Steel Company at Flemington, near Wishaw. He became Works Manager there, and later became a Director of the Colvilles Combine of companies. He represented the British Iron and Steel Federation all over the world, in places like Russia, Canada and Nigeria.

He was sent to Nigeria to break the news that their request to have a steel plant built there had been turned down. He must have impressed the Africans, for in his reply the Nigerian leader said how sorry they were to hear the bad news, but quoted a Bible verse from the Book of Proverbs: 'Faithful are the wounds of a friend'.

Willie married Ada McIlveen of Greenmount, Hillend Road, Lambhill. They lived in a Colville's house in Walter Street, Wishaw, and one evening they were sitting by the fire. Willie answered the phone, and had a lengthy talk to a friend. He sat down, and picked up his book. Shortly afterwards, his wife Ada was putting on her coat, and Willie said: 'Are you going out, dear?' Ada replied: 'Yes, I'm going out to phone you to see whether you'll talk to me for half an hour!'

Across the canal from Lambhill Iron Works were the ruins of Lochburn Foundry, near the West Highland railway line. The Foundry had been very busy with munitions manufacture during the First World War. My mother worked there making cores in the foundry. I was very grateful to Lambhill Iron Works. The frontage to their office had received some sort of terrazzo treatment, and the Strachur Street entrance provided a covered, smooth surface area after office hours in which to perfect the skills of 'wa' heidies' (wall headers) in which I was very interested. I became the runner-up, second only to the famous Bobby Carroll of Irvine Meadow and Celtic fame, in the annual Possil School Wa' Heidie Championships. I rate that achievement as highly as my Arbroath Midnight Bathers' Certificate.

The Chapel – The Church of St Agnes

If the Castle was the most imposing residence in Lambhill, the most imposing public building was the Roman Catholic Church of St Agnes. The inspiration behind this building was Father (later, Canon) James Cameron, who was a parish priest at Maryhill for fifty-five years. His Maryhill Mission included Lochfaulds and Lambhill. Father Cameron was a distinguished churchman who had battled against ill-health, and had a particular devotion to the thirteen-year-old child martyr St Agnes, who was executed around AD304. It was therefore fitting that the church was named in her honour. On Whit Tuesday, 23 May 1893, a thundery day, the memorial stone was blessed in the presence of a 2000-strong crowd. The church was opened on a beautiful summer day on 24 June 1894.

The first resident priest was Father Aloysius Godfrey, an Englishman educated by the Benedictine monks. He was succeeded by Father Edward Doody, and then by a strong man from Kerry, Father Patrick Houlihan, who came in 1888, and was well-known for his amazing energy, clear spiritual vision, and passionate support for the cause of total abstinence. Father Houlihan was transferred to Greenock in 1905, and was replaced in the same year by the godly Father James Mullen, a native of Gourock. My mother spoke in hushed tones of this quiet man of God, who served with great love and distinction. My mother's description of him was reminiscent of the Bing Crosby song:

'Father O'Flynn, you've a wonderful way with you, all the old sinners are wanting to pray with you,
All the wee children are wanting to play with you,
Here's a health to Father O'Flynn...'

Young and old alike loved this man. People remembered his involvement in the Cadder Pit Disaster, on 3-4 August 1913, when a fire broke out in the Carron Company's number 15 colliery, and twenty-two miners died, leaving twelve widows and forty-one fatherless children. Father Mullen doffed his silk hat for a borrowed miner's cap, and descended with the second rescue party, risking his life for others. There was an extraordinary wave of sympathy from the whole Glasgow area, and twenty thousand gathered on 22 March 1914 for the unveiling of a memorial stone in the cemetery.
Father Mullen was transferred to Pollokshaws in 1916, and died soon afterwards. The priest I knew about was Father Daniel Clancy, who served at Lambhill from 1948-1970.
There was some ambivalence in Protestant-Catholic relations in the area, as far as I was concerned. I had to 'cross the line' on my way home from Possil Primary and Secondary School, and face the challenging question: 'Are you a Proddy dog?' I became a very good runner to avoid the consequences. Nevertheless, we were good pals across the sectarian divide. The Morrow brothers, Jim, Tommy and Robin were among my best pals. I enjoyed playing football with them, and Jim Welsh, a fine player, 'Packy' Haggerty, the Devine brothers (Eamonn was an altar boy), and George MacDonald, a big stopper in defence. We knew about the Boys' Guild at St Agnes', and felt some resentment when they were off school for what they called

'a holy day of obligation', which seemed a bit of a mystery to us. Ma's family – the Halfpennys, Rowells, Butlers and MacIlroys, seemed to be what was called 'devout' in the Roman Catholic faith. The work at the Church of St Agnes continues.

The 'Caurs'

The Strachur Street terminus was the end of the line for Lambhill's trams. The trams had reached Lambhill by 1907. By 1920 Glasgow had developed a comprehensive system in accordance with the vision of James Dalrymple, General Manager of the then Glasgow Corporation Transport system. The tram routes extended to places with exotic names like Whiteinch and Auchenshuggle.

Glasgow Corporation had retained the Glasgow Tramway and Omnibus Company's system of colour differentiation, and the older generations of Glaswegians would refer to 'the blue caurs' (Number4B Lambhill and Linthouse) or the white, red, yellow or green 'caurs'. In 1938 the city moved from the colour coding of routes to the standardised livery of green, cream and orange. From 1946 onwards, the Number 22 tram connected Lambhill and Crookston. From 1943 onwards, the Number 31 ran from Lambhill to Hillington Road or Renfrew Cross, and was diverted to Carnwadric in 1949, and Merrylee in 1956. The 31 route made extensive use of the Coronation Cars with their green, cream and orange livery. The colour system created difficulties for some supporters of Glasgow Rangers, who preferred to walk to Airdrie when the 'Gers were playing there. It was a matter of principle – they would not travel on a 'green caur'! The sectarian divide persists – I recently met a boy who refused a bottle of limeade, because it was green.

Trams were safe in a city where children used the streets as their principal playground, and where it didn't matter that the Glasgow tram's average speed (7.91 miles per hour) came nowhere near their American streetcar counterpart (20 miles per hour). In fact, the trams were very suitable for drunks and children. The drunks (there were a few in Glasgow, although they functioned mainly on Saturday evenings), were adept at swaying at the same amplitude of vibration as the trams they were travelling on. Children became expert hoppers on and off the trams, learning from early infancy, it seemed, that you were safe as long as you were facing in the same direction as the tram was travelling. There was a nasty American rumour that Glasgow children were unaware of the function of their feet, because they lived and moved and had their being aboard tramcars. Trams rarely left their rails, or slipped their overhead cables. Trams were roomy. An inspector boarding a night service tram shortly after the bells one Hogmanay, found 103 passengers on board! Trams were cheap, and indigenous, unlike buses, which were at the mercy of imported oil and rubber. Trams were ubiquitous, covering some 270 miles of track. Passengers in the Glasgow area could go from the blackest of the Lanarkshire coalfields to the sylvan retreats of Loch Lomond, covering three counties.

What sights and sounds and smells the word 'tramcar' or 'the caurs' evokes in the minds of Glaswegians! We immediately envisage a multi-coloured metal monster, clanking and swaying its way into our hearts. We think of the winter draughts whistling along both decks from both ends. We think of the ticket collectors as 'clippies', who punched or clipped our tickets, or the 'duckies' (conductresses), who with swift hand and word administered direction and discipline to generations of Glasgow children. They were the stuff of jokes and cartoons, notably from Bud Neill of the Glasgow Evening Times, of 'Come oan, get aff" fame, or of the clippie swinging at right angles to the entrance pole as her tram swung round a corner on a windy day, with a member of the public shouting 'Hing oan, Captain Carlsen' (the brave captain of a freighter, who hung on for 12 days after the rest had abandoned ship in January 1952).

I was sometimes allowed to 'change the seats' at the terminus - the seat backs were moved in slots to match the tram's change of direction. Some clippies could have their laziness encouraged by accepting small boys' offer to 'change the screen', by leaning out of the upper deck window to operate the destination winder. One of my childhood dreams was falling headlong from the upper deck window of a tram, and never landing. Of course, the boys always had vested interests in so offering. The rewards were two-fold. The boys would ask for the elastic bands which held new rolls of paper tickets, and which were kept on the clippie's shoulder buckle. They could then be used with hairpins and wood for firing paper pellets in classrooms. The other spoil of toil for changing the seats on the upper deck was that we could gather the cigarette ends from the floor, to help in the production of 'home-made' cigarettes, using cigarette papers and tobacco from the gang's shag-tin. Lambhill children were always rather avant-garde. At the age of six or seven I was smoking home-made fags and playing pontoon with the lads!

The trams acted as a unifying factor, their metal life-line linking the areas of Glasgow life. I used to take the Number 22 to Cowcaddens, and get on the Underground to Copeland Road to see the famous Glasgow Rangers, or to Merkland Street for the circus or carnival at the Kelvin Hall. Trams were the last vehicles on the road in fog - fogs were fairly frequent in the industrialised city. When every other form of transport had given up, the ghostly rattle of the trams continued day and night. Trams were serviced, maintained and cannibalised in depots like Coplawhill, where Faither Mitchell was based. The Coplawhill Car Works occupied 23,000 square yards, and in its heyday the smiddy had twenty-five fires, with three gas-heated furnaces for heat treatment (quenching and tempering the steel). Some Glaswegians ransacked the Bible to find in the tramcars some fulfilment of the Old Testament's apocalyptic visions:

'Chariots dash wildly through the streets,
Rushing to and fro through the city squares,
They flash like torches,
And dart about like lightning' (Nahum 2:4).

On the other hand, to Glaswegians, the trams evoked memories of the old moral absolutes of life, dependable in the worst snow and fog, a fixed point in a world of turmoil - except when we were stuck in a traffic jam in Hope Street! I have to confess that when they reconstructed a short length of track for the Glasgow Garden Festival, and offered free tram rides, I jumped at the chance, and later cried like a baby because I had been on a Glasgow tram again, my mind flooded with childhhood associations! One of the best yarns in Lambhill lore about the trams concerned one reckless driver whose tramcar jumped the rails at the turning into Strachur Street, and ploughed into the front door of Ackie' de Marco's Ice Cream Parlour at the comer, bringing out the worst aspects of his hot Italian temperament.

Lambhill Evangelistic Mission
The pioneer of what became Lambhill Evangelistic Mission in Knapdale Street, the next street to the tram terminus, was Robert McLean, who had moved to Lambhill from Loch Lomond-side. He was invited to lead a Sunday School already in existence, and later the Maryhill United Presbyterian Church appointed Mr Dunlop, a

missionary, to conduct gospel meetings for adults each Sunday. Gospel interest was maintained by kitchen meetings, and some meetings in the Hibernians' Hall. Eventually, in March 1907, the present building was erected, and is still the only Protestant place of worship in Lambhill.

The Mission's stated object was 'the carrying on of mission work in the district known as Lambhill'. The Mission's affairs were to be managed by 'a Committee consisting of a President, a secretary, a treasurer, and other members shall be elected.'

One of the godliest people in the Mission was Mrs Annie Maclean McIlveen, who kept the grocer's shop. She regularly tore up her 'tick book', and forgave her debtors literally, testifying to the grace of God and His goodness in her life.

The Lambhill Gospel Silver Band was part of the life of the Mission from the earliest days. It started off with a quartet, and grew to about thirty members. It was part of the cultural legacy of 'music for the people' which arose from mining communities. The band always played only hymn tunes, marches and selections which included Gospel songs, and was an integral feature of their Christian witness in the village. They marched, helped at open air meetings, and went out on engagements in a wide area. On New Year's Day each year, they joined in the massed march witness of hundreds of Christians from the Tent Hall in Steel Street, Saltmarket, to Lewis' (now Debenhams) store in Argyle Street. The bandmaster in my childhood was the legendary figure Mr Alexander ('Soprano Jock', because of his prowess on the soprano cornet). He told the band their trouble was 'the want of too much practice', and on another occasion he told them they were 'improving scandalously'! The band had its own fund of stories, like the time the big drum rolled off a tramcar at the Maitland Street-Hope Street corner, or the time a cheeky youngster lobbed a half-brick down the E flat bass as they were marching in the Plantation district of Glasgow. At one band engagement in Paisley, a band member discovered to his consternation that he had brought his mother's 'store book' (Co-op payment book) instead of his book of band marches. Some of the band members used to take their girl-friends with them to engagements. A couple of lads arrived half-way through a meeting. They had been so pre-occupied with their girl-friends that they had travelled in the train to Greenock instead of Port Glasgow... Another fellow was so taken up with his girl-friend that he left his cornet on the upper deck of the tramcar. Such was the basic honesty of the good citizens of Glasgow that he was able to recover it in the Corporation Lost Property office in Bath Street the following Monday. One of the lads was torn between going to a band engagement and going to Aberdeen to support Rangers in a Scottish Cup game. The devil won, and when he came home, his mother told him the band-master had called to collect his trombone! We have no record of the harsh penance imposed, or whether Rangers won the match.

Enough of this badinage! A small group of bandsmen continues playing, ably led by Robert Glen. I will have more to say about the Mission later. It became the launching-pad for an astonishing number of people who were later to become what they called 'full-time Christian workers', like ministers missionaries and lay-preachers.

The Smiddy (Blacksmith's Shop)
Just across Balmore Road from Strachur Street, set back a little from the main road by an open area, was the local smiddy, located behind a 'memorial sculptor', who made headstones for the graves in the cemeteries.

There were still a fair number of horses on the road in my boyhood, and it was fascinating to catch the sights and smells of the blacksmith's shop and fire, and the work with these heavy, snorting animals. When there was a craze for metal hoops, or girds, and the cleeks to direct them, the blacksmith did a roaring trade in gird production. We had an enterprising leader called Danny Hattie, who got us to collect old car tyres, and do a track layout for gird races. He somehow made a concrete starting grid, painted off with starting stalls, and we were off!

The Shops
There weren't any shopping malls in Lambhill. Coming from town into Lambhill, the first shops were clustered around the Balmore Road-Kilfinan Street corner. Mallan's Pub, the booze recycling centre, was on the corner site. Faither claimed he used to put his stomach on the counter and say: 'Fill that!'.

I remember Hugh Brodie's Dairy halfway down Kilfinan Street. He had two sons with him in the milk delivery business, Ian and Evan. His custom extended with the building of Erradale Street and Eynort Street, and the major building scheme of Milton, which came later. My first job, aged 15, was to work with Mr Brodie as a milk boy, working from 6-8am. The old man drove a converted ambulance, and sang quietly most of the time, repeating the line: 'Will ye gang, lassie, gang tae the Braes o' Balquhidder?' The biggest shop in the village was the Lambhill Branch of Springburn's Cowlairs Co-operative Society at the foot of Kilfinan Street. Each customer had a 'store book', in which careful records of purchases were kept for the dividend ('the divvie') to be paid out quarterly or half-yearly. Sometimes the divvie reached 20%, and there was great rejoicing in the camp at the payout when it was marked in the book. Next to the main grocery store, but separate from it, there was a brick-built paraffin shed, with a strong metal door, with customers' cans lined up outside it – essential for those with paraffin lamps or stoves. There was great excitement when the paraffin shed went on fire, giving a spectacular show of smoke and flames. Groceries could be marked 'to get', and sometimes debts could be paid on Friday. This called for celebration, when we bought one-and-sixpence worth of 'tea-bread' (Paris buns, coffee buns etc.).

Round the corner in Balmore Road was the newsagent, Mr Guy Muir and wife, and further along, Tam Loudon had a fruit and veg shop, ably helped by his strong son, Campbell, and a delightful, affable lady called Alice. If you crossed the road, and walked along Balmore Road towards Knapdale Street, there was another row of shops, starting with the Post Office which also sold fruit, veg, and groceries. Papa Craig, and later on the McLean family – father John, and children Robert, Margaret, Jean and Gladys took over the Post Office as well as the shop. Further along was Hannah's Café, where we could buy ice-cream and sweets, and what Glasgow people call 'ginger' (flavoured carbonated drinks, for example Irn Bru). Later on, they built a fish and chip shop extension run by the Hannah's daughter Doreen (David Hannah's wife), and their daughter Margaret Beat.

Baird's café was located at the Balmore Road-Strachur Street corner. In my mother's time, it was owned by an Italian family, the De Marcos, and she worked for them. In our childhood, it was owned by the Baird family. I remember the old grandfather being driven in a pony and trap. They sold all the best sweets – soor plooms, rhubarb rock, and cinnamon balls, to name but a few. Early smoking activities involved cinnamon sticks, and you could roll your own cigarettes if they were willing to sell you Rizla cigarette papers.

Further down Balmore Road on the way to the canal bridge, there was a small fish and chip shop, in which one of my pals said 'Gimme a bag of chips. I don't want a pie – ma mammy says your pies are rotten!' His mother apologised later.

The Regions Beyond

If you ventured out Balmore Road beyond Lambhill Cemetery, there was a row of miners' cottages called 'Blackhill Raw', with a communal water supply from a standpipe at one end. The residents here included a matriarchal figure, Granny Evans, known locally as 'Easy' (Isabel) Fergie, who had a kind of 'club' of young men at Lambhill Mission for whom she knitted socks each Christmas. Willie and Jean Carlisle also lived in 1149 Balmore Road. Willie was an ex-miner. He was a champion trombone player, and bandmaster of Grove Street Institute band, and an ardent Partick Thistle supporter. The most illustrious resident of the Blackhill Row was John Oliver Evans, who was brought up by his Granny, became a minister of the United Free Church, serving at Dalry, Millerston, and North Woodside. He and his family emigrated to New Zealand, and the Very Reverend Doctor became Moderator of the Presbyterian Church of New Zealand. In his twilight years he has married Rita Ross, originally from the 'red building' in Balmore Road, and they are living happily ever after in Torrance.

A little further on out Balmore Road, there was a community of folk who occupied the Nissan huts vacated by servicemen when World War II ended. They were called 'the Squatters'. The Haggerty family, who later moved to number one Strachur Street were the first family to settle there, and there were some children from the 'Squatters' Camp' who became our friends at school.

You can see readily from the description that there were significant differences from today's society. We knew most of our neighbours, and parents felt free to let their children roam and play, happy to see them at mealtimes. There were not the haunting fears of paedophiles, or terror about e-numbers, allergies, and infections, which characterise our communities today. The standard of living was pathetically lower than today's, although the debt figures we hear about today make us wonder who has paid for what they seem to own! The work ethic seemed to be a stronger factor, where for today's people Jehovah-Jireh ('the Lord will provide') has become Jehovah-Giro…

CHAPTER FOUR –

BOYS AND GIRLS COME OUT TO PLAY

There was fun a-plenty for a Lambhill kid! At Lochside Cottage, I developed a love for the pigs, which were clever and amusing. Sometimes Faither would give me the runt of the litter in a shoe-box, and make me responsible for heating it up in the oven until it squealed, and feeding it with a baby's bottle until it was strong enough to fight its way to mother pig and her milk. In adult life, I once worked in a piggery in Bearsden, cleaning out pig-sties, and 'toilet-trained' little pigs to confine these activities to the corner of the sty, by simply leaving a little of their mess each day. Pigs are clever and generally amiable.

Faither used to buy day-old chickens and fatten them up. He once took a notion for a goose for Christmas dinner, which he obtained via one of his pals, and christened the gosling Barney. It was the noisiest, messiest creature you could have about the place. It grew to an awesome size, and when Faither trapped it in the wash-house to thraw its neck in preparation for Christmas, there was the most almighty racket - Barney squawking, and Faither cursing - until Faither shouted for the axe and put Barney out of his misery. We had two dogs - Bob a gentle big collie, and Judy, who was a cross between an Airedale and an Irish terrier. They operated a brilliant partnership hunting rats. When Judy died, Bob lay on her grave for two weeks, and would hardly eat anything. We had a ferret for a time, until it grabbed someone's thumb and its jaws locked on. The ferret was used to kill the rats we caught in a cage trap. We had a cat, and a nanny goat for a time. We also had a big rabbit called Percy.

One of the saddest moments of childhood was when I showed one of my pals a swallow's nest, with baby birds in it. My pal was so keen to have a swallow as a pet, that he took a baby swallow home in a sticky, empty syrup tin. There was a terrible guilt reaction to being party to the death of an innocent creature.

We had good fun rafting in the Pudge, a stretch of water behind Thom's yard in Knapdale Street. There were some trees around it. For us, a tree was an invitation for us to put up a rope swing, if we could find a rope, perhaps at the coup near our cottage. We also made rafts at Lochside, although we were wary of the family of swans in the little island in the centre of the loch. We had heard that a swan could break your arm with its wing, or peck your eyes out. The area beyond the tram-rails, and short of the Iron Works gates in Strachur Street was a favourite play area. The girls used the pavement for 'peever' or 'beds', by chalking boxes 1 to 8, and knocking the flat stone or peever through the range of numbers without touching the lines. (I hope that is a suitable explanation of hopscotch). The girls also played with skipping ropes, chanting strange rhymes as they skipped. We also had mixed games. Including both boys and girls, like 'release', in two teams, where one team chased and captured individuals, and guarded the den until some brave soul came running into the den shouting 'release'. We also played 'cigarettes', with all but one on the pavement at the start, and someone in the centre of the street shouting brand names of cigarettes, and the others who had chosen that brand name trying to hop past him or her to reach the opposite pavement.

Faither took me to a lot of football matches. He was a supporter of the Juniors, and Glasgow Perthshire in particular, whose home ground at Keppoch Park was adjacent to the tramcar depot. Facilities at the stadium, which could take 4,000 spectators, were rudimentary, to say the least. Some of the 'Shire players had gone on from wearing the black-and-white to do greater things in football. Bobby Campbell went to Falkirk and Chelsea, James Lawrence to Newcastle, Tod Sloan to Third Lanark, James Stark to Rangers, and Robert Thomson to St Mirren. The great local rivals were Ashfield and Petershill. 'Shire had won the Scottish Cup three times in fifteen years. In 1932 they beat Kirkintilloch Rob Roy 3-1 before a 13,000 crowd at Firhill. In 1941 they beat Annadale Thistle 3-1 before a 15,000 crowd at Tynecastle, and in 1944 they beat Blantyre Victoria 1-0 before a 32,000 crowd at Hampden. On each occasion, Faither performed the ritual of knocking over the tea table on his victorious return home.

As a boy, I was taken to all the Junior football grounds to see the 'Shire. The best stadium was the Kilsyth Rangers ground, and Shotts Bon Accord had a fine ground. The worst 'gluepot grounds' were where Maryhjll Harp and Duntocher Hibs played. The Pollok Juniors' ground had the problem of the ball being kicked into the River Cart. I saw wee Bobby Collins playing at Pollok before he achieved fame with Celtic, and the Steedman brothers turning out for Ashfield.

Lambhill had its own team of course, the Lambhill Amateurs, which achieved fame and notoriety in the West of Scotland Amateur League, and in the City and Suburban Amateur League. Match Committee meetings were held regularly in the Smiddy, near the pitch. The big stopper centre-half was Bobby Findlay, who always kept his head in a crisis. The three Thom brothers (Joe, Alex and Colin) were noted for their robust style of play, and when Joe was, in their estimation, unfairly treated, Lambhill withdrew from the League and didn't complete the season (the referee involved, a Mr Meldrum, was lucky to escape without being lynched). Alex Thom at centre forward had been a prolific goal-scorer, topping a hundred goals one season.

There were seasons of interest in different activities, for example, playing marbles, which involved simple strike games, and more complex ones knocking marbles out of a circle, or the game called 'Moshey', where the marbles were played in and out of three holes in the ground. Then there was a Dinky Toy phase, which I couldn't take part in because of lack of finance; a fishing season, which was again outwith my financial reach; and a gird-and-cleek era which I have mentioned.

When the new-house building was going on in Lambhill at the Eynort and Erradale Street area, there was a bit of inter-tribal warfare for a time, until we got the measure of each other. The weapons of warfare were slings (catapults). Branches from trees in a Y-shape formed the frame. Car or lorry inner tubes became a form of currency, and were cut into strips, tied into the tongues of old shoes or boots. The missiles (mutually agreed with the enemy) were pieces of chalk broken from the plentiful supply of plasterboard at the coup. There were some casualties, but nothing serious.

It was the cinema era, and there was plenty of choice. Lambhill had no cinema, but a short journey by tram took us to the 'Mecca' (later the 'Vogue') at the Balmore Road/Hawthom Street junction. There was the 'Avon' in Saracen Street, Possilpark, and further along the same tram route lay the 'Astoria' in Possil Road, also a couple of flea-pits called the 'Phoenix' or 'The Magnet' in Possil Road and the 'Endrick' in Sawmillfield Street, where it was said you were itching to

Marching with the Lambhill Band – 1950s

get in and scratching to get out. At the Cowcaddens there was the 'Grand', and it was only a short stretch to the big cinemas in town, like the 'Odeon'. There was what was called a 'Continental Cinema', called the 'Cosmo', in Rose Street, which screened Swedish films and specialist/classic films like 'The Seven Samurai', 'Rififi', 'Rashomon' and Disney's' Fantasia'. Later on, one of my workmates who dodged classes at College to go to Rose Street was said to have 'got his education in the Cosmo'.

Programmes changed twice a week, and some of the cinemas staged a Saturday matinee. The 'Mecca' attempted to introduce a kind of cheer-leader for matinees who led community singing, but the attempt failed because he was jeered at and pelted with unmentionables by the indescribables. The highlight of the Saturday matinees were the serials, where we were introduced to Superman, then Captain Marvel, whose wires were seen and jeered at in the flying sequences. There was also Flash Gordon (Buster Crabbe), 'hero of the twenty-fifth century', and his great opponent the Emperor Ming, whose acolytes clanked around like refugees from an ironmonger's shop.

There were some good films going about. The cowboy genre

starring John Wayne introduced us to the Wild West. Spencer Tracy's 'Doctor Jekyll and Mr Hyde' was worth watching, as was Peter Lorre's 'The Beast with Five Fingers', and Erroll Flynn's 'They Died with their Boots On' .Richard Widmark's 'Panic in the Streets', Orson Welles' 'The Third Man' and Trevor Howard's 'They Made me a Fugitive', were all good stuff. Great sympathy was evoked for those two big monkeys, 'King Kong' and 'Mighty Joe Young'. I suppose, on reflection, that the 'pictures', as we called them, gave us good practice at drama, because we sometimes 'acted them out'. I vividly remember us doing Charles Laughton's Captain Bligh and Quasimodo, and some of the James Cagney stuff, for example from 'White Heat'. Then of course, the films opened windows for us to the wider world, and American culture in particular.

CHAPTER FIVE –

'THE BEST WEE SCHOOL IN GLESGA'

'Oor School's a rerr wee school,
The best wee school in Glesga,
There's only wan thing wrang wi' it - The baldy-heided maister!
Goes tae the pub oan Saturday night, Goes tae the church oan Sunday,
Prays tae the Lord tae give him strength
Tae murder the weans oan Monday'.

The two senior, non-denominational schools in the district were 'Big Possil' in Ardoch Street, Possilpark, and 'wee Possil' between the two railway stations (Possil and Possilpark) in Balmore Road. In the drive for learning which followed Lord Young's Education Act, Possil Senior Secondary School was built in 1933-34, on the opposite side of Balmore Road from the stations, using fine red facing brick. Popular rumour said that the school was built with a view to conversion to a hospital were a war to break out. Possil was one of the few schools in Glasgow with a Primary Department integral to the plan. If you could imagine yourself standing facing the middle prong of a capital letter 'E' , then the central prong was the corridor linking the entrance hall and the office with the Physical Education Block (two gyms) at the other end. The top end of the 'E' was the Primary Department, and the remainder the Secondary School Departments, housed on two floors, with open corridors between classrooms. The open corridors overlooked two segregated playgrounds. Thus, it was possible to go right through the education process from age five to age seventeen, within one building. Feeder primaries increased the number in the Senior Secondary School to around 650 pupils. In our case, due to overcrowding in Primary VI and VII, we were moved out as Possil Primary annexe within Parkhouse Primary School. 'Big Possil' became Possilpark Junior Secondary School. Pupils were screened at Primary VII stage (age 11-12) by 'the Qually', or

Qualifying Examination, with the 'J's going to Junior Secondary and the 'S's going to Senior Secondary. There was also a verbal I.Q. (Intelligence Quotient) test at the Primary VII stage.

What can I say about Possil School? The infant school teachers were like granny figures. I must have shown promise (Ma, with the tinted glasses of motherhood claimed I could read the 'Dandy' comic before I went to school), because I was moved from Primary I to Primary III, and ever afterwards was one of youngest in any of my classes. The early years were uneventful, apart from the time our teacher decided that the boys should learn to knit. This of course was regarded as a direct assault on our masculinity! One of our classmates decided to sink his doubts about knitting by turning it into a race to be first finished with the scarf which was our first assignment. In fairness to the teacher, she warned us to bring out our knitting as soon as we had a problem. Unfortunately, the hole in row six of my classmate's work was not revealed until he swaggered out, first finished, to have the casting-off procedures performed. With great zest, the teacher started berating the boy and set about ripping out his work with an unhealthy zeal. The physical attacks on the teacher, then on the Headmaster, which followed, led to our classmate visiting the educational psychologist for two years. I sometimes thought that it should have been the teacher who was sent to the psychologist!

The big educational event of my Primary School career occurred in Primary VI, when we had our first male teacher, Mr Tommy Thomson. He started off by winning our undying gratitude by forming a football team, and entering us in the Glasgow Primary Schools' League. There was magic in the air that Monday after our first trial match when the team sheet went up on the notice board for the first time. In all weathers, teacher and team turned out for the weekly games. Some of the ash pitches were lethal, and the weather was often foul. I remember a game against Napiershall Street Primary being abandoned during the second half because of hailstones the size of marbles. We were 8-0 down, so we were fairly relieved. Valuable lessons had to be learned, as when Mr Thomson was refereeing one day, and sent our best player off for swearing at an opponent. He silenced the protests by saying 'If you swear on the pitch, you don't play in my team'. It all seems so far away and long ago when you see some of the antics on football fields today.

Mr Thomson was interested in the full range of educational experience. He drilled us mercilessly on mental arithmetic, in preparation for the 'Qually' (qualifying exam), using the figures of a clock which he chalked on the board. We did our 'forty sums in thirty minutes' routine in preparation for the 'Qually'. He taught us how to use the telephone, using blackboard sketches with Button' A' and Button 'B', and then did a thing no modern teacher dare do - he gave us his telephone number and told us to telephone him at the weekend, to prove we'd mastered the lesson. We built a township with matchboxes glued together. We made net bags, using string and a ruler. He told us about a big building in our district, where we could borrow books for the rest of our lives, as long as we kept taking them back, and plagued the life out of us until our parents signed the library application cards. For me, it was like Aladdin's cave being opened. My Auntie Nellie had given me a Bible when I was five, and Ma had bought me some books (my first book was called 'Sally the Sealyham'). When I had chickenpox she got some books for me from a lady in Lambhill. But Mr Thomson hit the jackpot! I read almost everything in Possilpark Library - the series about Sherlock Holmes, 'The Sea Urchin', 'The Scarlet Pimpernel', 'Biggles', 'Billy Bunter', 'Just William', 'Treasure Island', 'Kidnapped' and 'Catriona', Steinbeck's short stories, Hemingway's 'The Old Man and the Sea', Dickens, Scott's 'Legend of Montrose', 'White Fang', 'The Sea Wolf, 'Huntingtower', 'John MacNab' and so on.

Mr Thomson was at his best when fired up to teach us poetry. He used to sit on the edge of his desk, with his feet on the front desk. The holes in the soles of his shoes were a minor distraction. Little flecks of froth appeared at the edges of his mouth, as he read with great feeling 'Sea Fever', 'The Windmill', and 'The Highwayman'. He had an infectious enthusiasm for learning, and captured the imagination of his pupils, transporting them out of the drab and the tawdry, and the everyday. He belonged to the 'learn this off by heart by next week or I'll belt you' school of religious education, and so we had to learn Biblical passages like Psalm 1, the Beatitudes, and I Corinthians 13. Primary VI and VII came and went. I got an S1 for the Qualifying exam, and was the class prize-winner, and it was off to the Senior Secondary, to be a wee fish in the big pond.

We were told that education was the ladder to social and financial progress. As a poor boy, I never felt strongly about that, but developed much joy in learning for its own sake. The Nature/Nurture arguments which I heard later were interesting. I have found that my memories of childhood have been purified. I suppose that the memory tends to reject the unpleasant. As far as I am aware, neither of my parents ever visited my school. They were encouraging about my progress. Faither used to come and watch me playing football, but he always watched from a distance, and never came and spoke to Mr Thomson, which was a pity, but it could have been embarrassing. Mr Thomson certainly gave me a golden key to learning in an incarnational way, embodying the 'chase', and the joy, of knowledge. His composition subjects, like 'The Adventures of a Penny', helped to stretch our imaginations. My two books a week from the local library certainly developed what was there. The mathematical drills laid a foundation in number relationship which was helpful later. Our social skills developed in a mixed sex school. One of my teachers kept the seats beside two of the girls as a punishment for boy offenders, which could not have helped the self-esteem of the girls concerned. One of them had real difficulty with mathematical concepts, and counted the windows to answer her sums! When I discovered later at Jordanhill College what my I.Q. was, I wondered how this could have happened, because Ma was a simple soul of average intellectual ability. Faither was very brainy, but had to leave school to earn pennies to feed the family.

As well as the good footballers, there was a non-footballing Catholic boy among my friends who was known as 'Professor Fa-Fa', who seemed to be very widely read, and was often consulted for answers to technical questions.

Catholics and Protestants alike relished Hallowe' en as an enjoyable, seasonal, out-or-school activity. Hallowe'en provided a useful means of accruing capital, by dressing up and singing in other people's houses. Lochend House was a favourite, for old Jock Munro was unusually generous, and gave us half-a-crown each for singing 'The Crookit Bawbee' and other works of musical erudition.

My career in secondary school was seriously altered as a result of an experience of Christian conversion I had when I was twelve years and nine months old. I am going to write about my conversion, and my experience of secondary school in Chapter Six.

CHAPTER SIX –
'A GOOD-LIVING BOY'

The religious input in my life so far had been minimal. Auntie Nellie, the family Hallelujah, had taken me to a few Salvation Army meetings when I was a kid. I had read the Bible she gave me as far as Genesis Chapter 5, which was too full of 'and he died' for my liking. I also had a short period of attendance at Lambhill Mission Sunday School, but gave up on the grounds of my inconsistency. My Sunday School teacher had an apple tree, and it didn't seem right somehow to sit in her class on Sundays, and rob her apple tree through the week. There was also a bit of moral guilt about stealing cider from the Corry's Belfast Waters bottling plant, where we used to climb the fence, knock in the bung of a barrel, and go home very drunk. My guilt was tinged with a dash of self-preservation, because sometimes I was so drunk that I was scared of falling in the Forth and Clyde canal on the way home. People who question me about drinking and smoking are sometimes surprised to learn I gave up smoking at age seven, and drinking at age eight! Since I had heard people referring to God as 'Our Heavenly Father', I thought God must be a bit like my father - a big Tough Guy out to get me. Assemblies in the school gym or the local parish church had failed to grab my attention, as the minister was a nice old gentleman, but extremely un-dynamic. I had learned a good few verses of the Bible, usually out of motives of fear. Mr Thomson belonged to 'learn these verses by heart by next week or I'll belt you' school of religious education.

Saturday evenings, especially in winter, posed a problem for the footloose Lambhill lad. Faither was at the pub, and Ma was engaged in woman-speak with her pals. We used to hang about the tram terminus, freezing. One night, one of the lads suggested going to the 'bun-fight', as he called it at the local Mission Hall. I learned later that the official title was' A Gospel Tea Meeting'. There was a chucker-out on the door, a careful wee man who made sure that you put at least three pence in the collection plate, for which the return was a hot cup of tea and an iced bun. The Mission Hall was clean, well-lit and warm. A painted banner text above the platform area read: 'Seek Ye First the Kingdom of God' (Matthew 6:33). In addition to the tea, there was hearty singing from a small book kindly supplied. I found the songs interesting, if a bit strange. 'Come away to Jesus, let elusive trifles go', they sang, and I had this mental picture of jellies jumping about. They also sang 'you will find a solace there', which I took to be a mis-print for a shoelace. The chairman also prayed to God with curious language: 'Bless the great army of sick ones' he prayed, and I envisaged guys on crutches marching down the road. Every week there was a different 'deputation' as they called it. There were male voice choirs, Gospel bands, duettists, 'readers' (self-styled elocutionists) who recited poems about old violins and other sundry objects, people who played musical saws, and so on. Once there was a wee lady who played a harmonium and sang 'And the Ship Went Down', while her assistant showed 'lantern-slides' of the sinking of the Titanic. Here on one of the tinted slides was a gentleman perishing under the surface of the Atlantic Ocean, while still wearing a top hat!

The final act in each programme was 'the preaching of the Gospel'. Someone would give a message from the Bible, usually about Jesus and what He did for us by dying on a Cross. It was this aspect of the evening that intrigued me, and kept me coming long after my pals had given up. It seemed as if someone had tipped off the preachers about me as a rotten wee sinner. They spoke about sin and forgiveness and Christ's return to judge everyone. They spoke about the Bible as the Word of God, and the need to repent, and how Christ could change our lives. Now although at age thirteen I had not been involved in syndicated crime, I was a liar and a thief and a blasphemer. I occasionally got into scrapes, one of which involved a Lambhill classmate in primary school. He had 'found' a pound note (in his mother's purse, perchance?), and wanted to treat me to the cinema. We boarded the tramcar after school, and got off at the nearest cinema. Before going in, he bought thirty cigarettes. In the austerity of the post-war period, you had to buy foreign cigarettes before you could purchase more conventional brands. Stewart bought twenty 'Pasha' (a Turkish brand, made from cow-dung I believe), and ten' Prize Crop', and we smoked ourselves silly in the cinema, had ice-creams at the interval, and took the tram home. I remember a sense of foreboding as I walked along the canal bank. The first thing that struck me as I entered the living-room was a scrubbing brush, flung with power and accuracy by Ma, and when Faither got out of bed to go on the nightshift, and piled in with a few heavyweight blows, I knew not to do that sort of thing again. I have occasionally reflected how much you could get for a pound in those days - return tram fares, entrance to the cinema for two, ice-creams, and thirty cigarettes.

Shortly before attending the Mission, I had had a long and successful run as a truant brought to a sudden halt. Ma had always signed my 'sick notes' when I was absent from school. I got a pal to be 'ghost writer' for Faither, which worked well until one day I needed a note and my scriptwriter was unfortunately absent! Swift detection followed and it was off to the Headmaster for a good lecture about the stupidity of a clever boy truanting from school, etc. I respected the Headmaster, because he said if I looked him in the eye and promised never to truant again, he would not give me a thrashing.

The preachers at the Mission seemed to know about all of this. Over a period of weeks, I felt very guilty and responsible about my spiritual state before God. I realise that critics would say that the preaching was inducing guilt in a young, thirteen-year-old boy.

The last stage in my weeks of misery came one Saturday evening when the preacher man didn't fit my distorted image of manliness. He had soft hands and a high-pitched voice, and a handkerchief up his sleeve! He was everything Faither was not. Everything in my natural disposition would reject the idea that this man could speak authoritatively with reference to my condition. He spoke simply and directly about the love of God in Jesus Christ. The most telling sentence in his talk was when he said that if anyone of us were the only sinner in the world, Christ would still have come to earth to die for us. That hit me like a sledgehammer. There was no soft music, no big auditorium, no large crowd, no sugary invitation. I didn't speak to anyone. I went along the canal bank quietly, went upstairs to my cold bedroom, and asked Christ to receive me and forgive me, to become my Saviour and Lord. It took me months to figure out the next move. I had no emotionally melting moment, no tears, just a quiet certainty that my act of daring in praying to God had produced a definite, internal result. I could grit my teeth and live now on the strength of it. This was the last Saturday in January, 1952. I notice that my school report card for the previous summer term shows twenty absences (truanting).

There are a few things to be said in retrospect. First of all, no psychologist or rationalist is going to talk me out of my experience. Ronald Knox wrote, 'Beware of a man with an experience.' The

American evangelist Billy Sunday was asked by an interviewing panel how he came to be so sure of his salvation, and he said, 'I was there when it happened, and I ought to know.' I agree. Secondly, although there was a period of unhappiness, it was not, I believe, due to guilt-inducing techniques used by the preachers. These were ordinary working men on the whole, unskilled in manipulating audiences. I would prefer to say it was a God-induced work of gradual conviction of my sin and need of God. Jesus said that those who were forgiven much, loved much. I still maintain that a sense of sin is a healthy thing, and that the motivation for 'making a commitment', to use the modern, man-centred terminology, is better and deeper when it is based on a sense of need for God's forgiveness rather than a desire to be happy and fulfilled. Although there was no one to explain it to me at the time, I have never doubted that God saved me that night. I have also had a strong conviction that the One who began a good work in me would bring it through to completion until the day of Jesus Christ. Hymn-writers express it better than I can.

'Soon as my all I ventured on the atoning blood, The Holy Spirit entered, and I was born of God'.

'My name from the palms of His hands Eternity cannot erase,
Impressed there forever it stands
In marks of indelible grace.
Yes! I to the end shall endure,
As sure as the earnest is given,
More happy, but not more secure,
The glorified spirits in heaven'.

On reflection in adult life, I am sure that the only thing we bring to the table, so to speak, in the matter of our salvation, is our sin. Even the faith I exercise to trust Christ is God's gift. The apostle Paul wrote in Ephesians chapter 2 verses 4,5,7 and 8: 'Because of His great love for us, God, who is rich in mercy, made us alive with Christ even when we were dead in transgressions - it is by grace you have been saved....For it is by grace you have been saved, through faith – and this not from yourselves, it is the gift of God – not by works, so that no one can boast. To use the perhaps out-dated illustration, it is like the starter-motor of a car. We have to acknowledge the initial work of the Holy Spirit to make us aware of our need of God, like the starter-motor, and then the other features of 'the engine' come into play, like our repentance and faith.

As a post-script to the meeting I attended, I later wrote to the soft-voiced preacher, and thanked him for his visit to Lambhill that night. I also met him later, in the congregation when I was preaching at Helensburgh Baptist Church. Imagine my surprise to learn within the past year that he was still alive, and Jean and I were able to visit him in a nursing home on our way home from Dumfries, aged 95!

I began private Bible reading and prayer. My conversion was based to a large extent on the message of the grace of God preached from Scripture, in the company of God's people. On the other hand, in terms of my response, it seemed to be a private matter. When I had to face what was called 'the assured results of critical scholarship', I found myself a doughty defender of the inspiration and authority

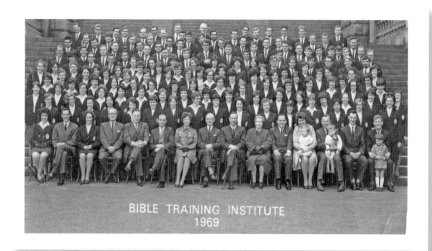

Bible Training Institute – 1969

of the Bible. God's work of grace in my life gave me a pro-Bible bias, which enabled me to accept the whole Bible as 'God-breathed' (2 Timothy 3: 16), and suspend judgment on the unexplained parts while diligently seeking explanations. John Calvin said that the Spirit-given certainty that the Bible is the Word of God is something that every Christian experiences.

What happened was confirmed to me in July the same year when I attended a Scripture Union Camp, led by James 'Boss' Meiklejohn, who slotted everything into place for me in his tent meetings, so that when I went back from camp, I made my Christian faith public to my parents and pals, started attending Sunday worship, and got involved in the Christian Endeavour Movement. Faither had been astonished when I asked to go to S.U. Camp, but he made the money available. He was surprisingly muted when he learned that I had become a Christian. Although he never modified his own swearing rate, he used to say to his pals, 'Watch whit yer sayin' noo - Geordie's become a good-livin' boy.'

'My Teacher Taught Me How To Live'
There is an old saying, which is rather unfair as a comprehensive description, but it contains elements of truth -'My mother gave me life; my teacher taught me how to live.' In Secondary School, we were to a large extent being prepared for life in the workaday world. The period after my conversion to Christ was a very interesting one. There was a change of pals. My best two friends in school 'dumped' me because I 'had become a snob'. In our school, to some people, if you wore underwear you were a snob! I was to meet up with one of my good buddies later. Some of my other pals got into serious problems in later life. One of them smashed a 'screwtap' (Glasgow description for a beer bottle with a threaded hard top) over the head of someone in a pub disagreement, which resulted in imprisonment for attempted murder. My new pal David has been a loyal friend over the years. He's the kind of person, and his is the kind of friendship which C.S. Lewis describes in his book The Four Loves under the explanation of 'storgia' (affection). Our friendship persists despite barriers of time and distance. We meet only occasionally now, but when we do, our friendship just slips into gear again as it was all those years ago. It is like coming home and putting on your favourite slippers. We played a lot of tennis together, and golf, and swam, and generally put the world right as in a way we developed a Christian interpretation of the world around us.

Growing up together in a mixed-sex school brought all the usual adjustments to our developing sexuality. It also brought the opportunity to relate to the girls around us in class and leisure, and to come to terms with their development too. We learned the difference between the formal and the informal, and how to be pals without forming exclusive friendships. My first attempts to swim took place with a girl's help, as I have described earlier.. There wasn't any sex education as part of our school programme, but we devised policies of survival in after-school hours. It is hard to imagine in relation to modern attitudes to 'gays', but we had in the district two characters in particular who were marked out by us as homosexual, and communal protection policies warned us against fraternising with these two, older, men in the cinema, or elsewhere, in case they attempted to force their attentions on us, especially up closes.

What about the teachers in Possil Secondary School? Only the names have been suppressed, to protect the innocent. My English friends were amazed to learn later on that in Scotland, teaching was a graduate profession, and because of streaming procedures, in general the top classes always got the Head of Department, who was almost invariably an Honours graduate. Therefore, a poor boy who made it to secondary school, if he obtained an S1 pass in the 'Qually', could go through school taught by the elite among the teaching staff. A number of the staff had been recruited to teach after War service. One teacher had served in the Far East, and had to be off for a few days occasionally because of bouts of malaria. Another one had been a navigator in a Lancaster bomber which had been shot down, and this had left a legacy of nervous problems. We had a maths teacher who was off ill for a lengthy period, and his classes were covered by all and sundry, including a music teacher with a soporific voice. As he droned on one day (the period after lunch seemed to be the sleepiest time), he obtained the agreement of one of my classmates that the angle he was pointing at was equal to the camel's hump, for which the boy was promptly belted.

Later on, this music teacher was replaced by a lady teacher who was immediately christened 'Hiawatha' by some, and 'Geronimo' by others, on the grounds of her dark and wrinkled skin, her centre parting, with the two parts drawn into a bun at the back, held by a wooden clasp, and her dress sense, which favoured autumnal colours, diaphanous blouses, and what the pupils called 'brass plaques' holding things together in the cleavage department. She was an inspiring enthusiast, looking for 'good songs that the boys can sing'. Under the previous incumbent, we were singing things like 'Nymphs and Shepherds', and 'I know a bank whereon the wild thyme grows' (the Forth and Clyde Canal bank didn't seem to fit the bill for that). Now we were singing 'The Maple Leaf Forever', 'Men of Harlech', 'Santa Lucia', 'The Lorelei', and other songs intrinsically satisfying, while lending themselves as good material for parodies. She also got us dragooned into attending concerts given by the Scottish National Orchestra at St Andrew Halls near Charing Cross.

The art teacher, who had us drawing cones and rectangles until we were sick, retired and was replaced with an enthusiast who taught us perspective, and showed us good films, such as the Norman MacLaren films, 'Boogie Doodle', and serious art films on the life of Van Gogh and one on the life of Leonardo da Vinci called 'The Tragic Pursuit of Perfection'.

In the Maths department, we got a small, no-frills man who gave examples on the board, and then went round the class giving individual tuition. He was good at explaining things and correcting errors. I won the Maths prize in sixth year.

In English, we had a bizarre individualist, a bachelor who wore thorn-proof tweed suits, thick check shirts, and Munro-spun ties. His shoes were highly polished black brogues, bulled-up in Army style, and he walked with a peculiar, bouncing, long-legged gait. He was a splendid teacher of Shakespeare, especially 'Macbeth', a great enthusiast for 'Tam O'Shanter', and gave a brilliant explanation of 'The Ancient Mariner', and 'Sohrab and Rustum'. Our English teacher had favourite phrases, like' Why don't you give up opium?!', used especially after lunch in Senior school, when some of us had been out delivering milk, running the streets at 6 am. He sometimes put boys in the cubby-hole under his desk, with the command, 'Into your kennel, Dog!' He then pulled in his chair, and taught seated, kicking his prisoner (gently) to elicit an occasional bark. I have sometimes wondered how men like this would have survived in the modern educational scene. Sadly, this fine teacher ended his days in psychiatric care. There wasn't an ounce of malice in him. He loved teaching, and was fond of his pupils. He cried when we gave him a silk cravat when he was leaving Possil to take promotion elsewhere.

In French and Latin we had an ex-despatch rider of World War II, a bachelor with a bright red countenance and the most nicotine-stained fingers you ever did see, who boasted a one hundred percent pass record in 'Higher' French year after year. (I realise that this would not be a large number of pupils in a school like ours). He was one of the few teachers I have met who employed a negative marking system - one mark off for a wrong noun ending, two for a wrong gender, three for conjugating a verb with 'avoir' instead of 'etre', and so on. (He told me in front of the class that if I went to France with that French accent, I'd be arrested as a Russian spy!) When submitting homework, the secret was to try to get your homework jotter near the top of the pile, because he got so mad by the time he got to the end of a batch, that his red biro pen was liable to go through the paper! In Science, the teacher had a bad heart and could not even summon up strength to go to the staff-room at intervals. He retired hurt, and was replaced by a rollicking, leather-faced individual whose opening gambit was to gather us round his table in the lab, and make the following speech: 'The last cove told me you are all rubbish. I refuse to believe that. Next March, some of you will sit Higher Science. You are the sheep. Some of you will sit Lower Science. You are the goats. The rest of you are vermin, and I'll play any of you at badminton for a pound any time you fancy yourself.' He was a first-class teacher, especially in chemistry.

The Physical Education teacher had a reputation for cruelty and brutality. He belted the latecomers, who formed around him in a circle each Monday, and filed past him twice for the belt. He rewarded a boy who was rather languid in his approach on the football pitch, by making him run round the pitch for an hour. He seemed to slow up deliberately when getting ready to take us on board the tramcar for swimming at Woodside Baths (we walked from the Garscube Road/North Woodside Road junction). When some of us pre-empted matters by jumping on the tram which arrived before he had, he told us to get ready for swimming, and line up in our trunks to be individually interviewed in the freezing-cold public baths, then made us take a cold shower and report next morning at school for two of the belt each. Double pneumonia all round . . .

As the years passed, badminton and other skills improved. I became Junior School sports champion, member of the school football, athletics and badminton teams, chairman of the Debating Society, and School Captain. Christian training at the Mission developed confidence through the Christian Endeavour meetings, in preparing papers, running committees, and speaking in public. By the time I left school, I had a Third Year Certificate, and a Scottish Certificate of Education with 'Higher' grade passes in English, French, Mathematics, Science and History, and a pass in Arithmetic.

In 1955, the American evangelist Billy Graham hit Glasgow. He came with his team to the Kelvin Hall for six weeks. Crowds flocked from all over the country, and even the news-vendors caught the atmosphere and the excitement. I remember one stout chappie who sold the 'Glasgow Evening Citizen' shouting at the top of his voice outside the Kelvin Hall, 'Erra Billy Graham Speshul! Photies o' the great evangelist!' There was a Schools Rally, when all the non-denominational schools were given the afternoon off, and transport was provided for us to attend at the Kelvin Hall and hear Billy preach and Cliff Barrows play his trombone. The Billy Graham 'Crusade', as it was called, had a profound effect. Several of our classmates responded to the invitations. It was an unusual time, when Christianity was being talked about on the tramcars. Billy Graham gave an invitation nightly to 'get up out of your seat'. Many people continued in the Christian way long after the final event in the Crusade, a Rally in Hampden Park. was over, I still meet people who remember these days with enthusiasm,

My first introduction to work came before I left school, working as a milk delivery boy with a local dairy first, then with Scottish Farmers Dairy in Possil Road, beside the Astoria Cinema, and finally with Cowlairs Co-operative in Kemp Street, Springburn. The hours were standard for part-timers in all three – 6 until 8 am, for fifteen shillings a week, The tips in the Scottish Farmers round brought an extra thirty-five shillings a week. With the Co-op, it was possible to go full-time during the summer holidays – 5 am until I pm, for £4 a week (no tips!). Our driver on the Milton round was an official in the Orange Lodge, who trained us like slaves in the week before the Black Walk. The trick was that he was allowed to finish when his round was finished that Saturday. We ran like stags that morning, and delivered 28 crates of milk by 8 am. We returned after breakfast to discover that the Springburn driver was off, and instead of a leisurely tour of the Co-op dairies as normal, we had the dreaded Springburn round - nearly all tenement closes - to do. The Springburn round was a killer, and included 103 half-pints, mainly to spinsters or widowed ladies in the top flat! For those interested in social history, apparently people who wanted a quiet life gradually moved upstairs as houses became available. The other interesting point was that there were people in those far-off times who could exist on half-a-pint of milk a day! Some of the closes were reeking with the pungent odour of cats' urine, so things were a bit unpleasant. The only area without tenement closes was a section known as 'the blocks' - railway workers' houses connected by a kind of gangway. Some of the boys engaged in illicit trading, secreting bottles of milk by laying them flat between the upright bottles in the case, and covering them quickly with another case.

School had been a happy experience. Like the pebbles on the beach, we knocked the rough edges off one another in the context of compulsory contact. Sometimes we found ourselves involved in inter-departmental activities, such as when we put on an open-air performance of Shakespeare's 'A Midsummer Night's Dream', with Art, Housewifery (Home Economics, who designed and sewed costumes), PE and chiefly English departments sharing together. The annual sports at Firhill Stadium (home of the famous Partick Thistle, the Maryhill Magyars) were good experiences, as were the school Christmas dances. The school contact with adults was useful, in learning command structures, and finding varied forms of leadership styles from those who taught us.

We moved house in 1952 to Possilpark, in Stoneyhurst Street, to a ground-floor flat in what was known as 'the good end'. The coup at Lochside had been finally filled in, and the Cadder scheme was to be built. I understand that our cottage was not demolished, but filled over in the hollow where it stood.

There was a radical re-adjustment for Faither. He was away from his beloved pigs and the open spaces around Lochside Cottage. He fenced in his wee bit of ground, protected it like a medieval citadel, barbed wire included, and made the best of his new garden. He made friends with the family in the prefab opposite, and an enemy in the drunken loudmouth who lived one storey up in the next close. This man's house was so bereft of furniture and carpets (he had used all the skirting board and every door except the front door and the bathroom door for firewood), that his voice echoed around the closes as he berated his wife and family. There was no connection between the volume of sound he generated and his physical frame. In Glasgow terms, he was a wee skelf (splinter) you could have spat peas through. One day in the mysterious providence of God, Faither and I were passing down the street just as this man emerged from his house. In a single bound, Faither grabbed this man by the neck of his shirt, lifted him up until eyeball contact was established, told him that he was a night-shift worker and that if our neighbour wakened him again he would break his back, and then dropped him like a rag doll. He was quiet for at least a week.

Outwith school, I was finding alternative models in the communal life of the Mission. Shortly after my conversion, a lady gave me a parcel of clothes, and gently spoke with me about the possibility of my mother being offended, in which case, I had just to return them. They belonged to her son, who was in my year at school. Other folk invited me into their home for supper after the evening service, where

I found warmth and a welcome, a table with a lace tablecloth laden with lovely food, a roaring fire in the sitting-room, and there was a sing-song round the piano. They also unwittingly introduced me to a new concept - saying grace before meals! I liked what I found in the Christian homes of these kind Mission people, and resolved, if I ever found anyone willing to take up the challenge of having me, I would set up a home like that. Since these boyhood experiences, I have always encouraged Christians to show hospitality, and provide havens and alternative models for everyone, but particularly for people young in the Christian faith, and coming from non-Christian homes.

1955 and 1956 were difficult years. Jim was away in the forces. He had joined the Army for a twelve-year engagement in 1947. In the spring of 1955, Ma almost died. I have written about this earlier.

Faither had a health problem in 1956. He lost his voice, and after investigation in Oakbank Hospital (in Baird's Brae across from the Astoria cinema), he was moved to Ruchill Hospital. In August 1956, Faither died. His cancer of the throat reduced him to a shadow of his former self in six weeks. I organised the funeral to Lambhill Cemetery, although we had difficulty getting someone to bury him. A friend of Lambhill Mission did the needful. After his death I had a sense of guilt for what I regarded as my failure to witness effectively to him, but I later came to leave the issues of his life and death with the Lord.

CHAPTER SEVEN –
'DOING THE HALLS'

The Scripture Union camp I attended moved me on in Christian commitment. In September 1952, I joined the Lambhill Gospel Band, an outreach of Lambhill Evangelistic Mission, which had been founded in 1895, and had grown from a brass quartette (two cornets, a tenor horn and a euphonium) into a brass band. At the time I joined, there were about twenty-five male members. Their motto was 'Make a joyful noise unto the Lord'. The qualification for joining was that members had to be able to give public testimony to the saving grace of God in their lives. You did not have to be able to play a musical instrument, which was obvious in my early efforts to blow the cornet I had been given. Faither's response when he heard the infernal din I was making was typically pragmatic: 'Stick in, son - we might get a new hoose oota this!'

It was through the work of the Band that I cut my teeth as a preacher a few years later, speaking at open-air meetings, and 'giving testimony' as they called it, while the Band was fulfilling its engagements at churches and mission halls around the country. Over the years, the Band had developed its own lore, like the story of the bandsman in the early days of the Glasgow Underground who went round full circle twice when he went past his intended stop.

The Band had associations with the many mission halls of the Glasgow area. Many of these were built to cater for specialist areas of life when Glasgow was at its zenith as a port, a railway centre, and a key industrial base in the British Empire. There were railway missions at Maryhill (Cumlodden Drive), Springburn (Vulcan Street), Townhead (Tennent Street), and Oatlands (Logan Street).

Artizans' Hall (known locally as 'Munzie's Mission' because it was founded and led by him) lasted from 1891 until 1971. It was located in the Kelvinhaugh area (Teviot Street) and catered for ordinary folk. During the Depression, there were 'Mufflers Meetings' held each Friday. One of my friends encountered a language difficulty when he visited America, and told them about these meetings. To the Americans, a muffler was a car exhaust pipe rather than a woolly scarf...

Mr Alex Morrison, who read the Bible right through over sixty times, was a well-known preacher from Artizans. He began as a telegraph boy, and rose to a senior position in the Post Office. Many of these men were educated at what they called 'The Holy Ghost Bible School' through reading the Bible.

Paddy Black's Mission (hundreds attended their Sunday School Trip), and the Douglas Children's Mission in the Plantation district, did a great work on the south side of the city. There was a flourishing Foundry Boys' Mission in Tharsis Street, Garngad, near Blochairn Steel Works, and the Canal Boatmen's Institute in Port Dundas. The last-named place was neither large (the main hall seated about 270), nor expensive (it cost £3,000 to build). It was a striking building, demonstrating great imagination in its use of its corner site, with an attractive, well-proportioned clock tower, modelled on that of the Old University, with the ogee cap common in Scottish seventeenth and eighteenth century buildings. Scholars have discovered within the last generation that although John Keppie was the architect, there is definite evidence that the young Charles Rennie Mackintosh, his junior, had a major influence on the building. This was, sadly, not enough to spare the building from demolition in 1967 to make way for the northern section of the ring road. The leader in my era was Mr Johnny Houston.

There were specialist missions for seamen in Glasgow, near the River Clyde, notably the Seamen's Bethel in Eaglesham Street (architect R.A. Bryden), which was demolished in May 1971. The Bethel was built to cater for sailors landing on the south side of the River Clyde, and had recreation and coffee rooms on the ground floor, and a chapel seating 500 upstairs. The Bethel had a Gospel Silver Band. The Seamen's Chapel, in Brown Street, Anderston, was north of the River Clyde and had extensive halls and a large chapel area. The Church of Scotland Lodging House Mission in East Campbell Street did a valuable work for the homeless and destitute. The Grove Street Institute in the North Woodside area near Garscube Road did a splendid work to help the poor (they used to talk about 'ameliorative ministries'). They supplied clothing, footwear and food for the poor. The northern area of the city had Mission Halls at Braid Street, and Bardowie Mission in Possilpark (known locally as 'Allan's Mission'). There was an unusual Mission in the south side of the city - the Gorbals Medical Mission, founded in 1867 to do medical missionary work among Glasgow's poor, to support the training of medical missionaries, and to encourage the missionary spirit among Glasgow's medical students. The Glasgow Royal Infirmary attracted students from all over the world. (A medical 'wag' joked that the Continental students came to practise their embroidery at Casualty on Saturday nights, and they didn't even need to give an anaesthetic, as the pubs had already provided that!). In 1883. the Hall and Dispensary was moved from Moncur Street to Oxford Street in the Gorbals, although the Moncur Street work continued. In 1973, the Mission moved to Nicholson Street. The work was led for many years by a wonderful Hebrew Christian, Miss Celia Goldfein, and Dr May Oastler was doctor in attendance.

The Tent Hall in Steel Street, Saltmarket, was the 'flagship of the fleet' among Glasgow's Mission Halls. It had been built in the aftermath of D.L.Moody's mission in a huge tent pitched on Glasgow Green in the 1870s. The Tent Hall was a spacious auditorium, with upper and lower areas. There was no escape from gospel application. Those who surreptitiously glanced at the clock inevitably saw the text above it, 'It is Time to Seek the Lord'. The Tent Hall had a free breakfast for the poor on Sunday mornings, a free dinner for children on Sunday afternoons, and a programme throughout the week busy enough to satisfy any evangelical activist. In later life, I was asked to speak at the oddly-named 'Spiritual Tonic Service', held about 3.30pm. I realised what the tonic was for one tramp at least. He threw his head back, and snored loudly throughout my carefully-thought-out message.

Glasgow City Mission had various Mission Halls throughout the city, including the work in Coalhill Street, Camlachie (led for years by Mr Danny Carmichael), and Wyndford in Maryhill Road (led for years by Mr Jimmy Wood), as well as a thriving work in Govan. There was the Tolbooth Mission, Duke Street Mission (which was what used to be called' 'a shop-front mission'; it continues in the same building format in High Street), and the Bethany Hall in Bridgeton, in Bernard Street for many years, but later located in the YWCA premises in Muslin Street.

Glasgow United Evangelistic Association (which included the Tent Hall, the Bethany Hall until the 1970's, the Cripple Children's League and the Fresh Air Fortnight) controlled the wider perspective on evangelism in the city. The great tri-partite building in Bothwell Street - Y.M.C.A./Christian Institute/Bible Training Institute – provided a focus. The Fresh Air Fund paid for seaside holidays for disadvantaged Glasgow children, and the Cripple League had a special remit for the physically handicapped. Many of Glasgow's residents had suffered injury in the heavy industry around the city. Many had been mal-nourished, so that the city had produced a higher-than-expected percentage of what were unkindly called 'wee bowly bachles' (diminutive, bow-legged, misshapen people). A well-known Glasgow phrase was 'God bless yer rickets' (rickets was the malformation of the bones, particularly the leg bones, through malnourishment, particularly calcium phosphate deficiency).

The Glasgow United Evangelistic Association used to hold a weekly lunch-time meeting, called 'The Noon Meeting', on Mondays, in the Christian Institute. It was basically a praise meeting and a reports meeting on the Gospel fruit which had been harvested over 'the weekend's work'. There was also an inspirational message from a guest speaker.

The Tent Hall used to lead a united march of witness every New Year's morning, led by Christian bands, from Steel Street in the Saltmarket to Lewis's in Argyle Street and back. Hundreds of Christians from all over the city used to gather for this. A word about the workers. The Tent Hall had many gifted leaders in its history, men like P.T. McCrostie, known as 'the man who walked backwards'. He obtained this nickname because of this habit which he adopted when leading open-air marches. Peter McCrostie was a strong and happy man, who gave away his coat to poor men many a time. His wife was a tiny, quiet-spoken and determined lady who used to target prostitutes for Gospel ministry, bringing them home from Glasgow Green for baths, meals, tender loving care, and Christian witness. After Peter's death, Mrs McCrostie went with her daughter Petrina to Peru, where they served as missionaries for years.

Jock Troup had strong associations with the Tent Hall during his time of training at the Bible Training Institute, and his Superintendency. He was a cooper to trade, born in Fochabers, and brought up in Wick. He was converted during the First World War while serving on the drifter 'Strumbo', and called by God to be a preacher one day when he was travelling through Aberdeen en route to Yarmouth. He had powerful shoulders and a voice to match. When he spoke in the open air meetings at Glasgow Cross, he could be heard at Lewis's in Argyle Street. He had huge hands, and could lift a fully-inflated football easily in one hand. God used him in what can only be called revival blessing across the coastal towns of the North-East of Scotland. The blessing evident among the fisher-folk travelled backwards and forwards between the Scottish fleet and the English ports, Lowestoft and Yarmouth. He was also a powerful singer, and while in Glasgow he held open-air meetings at the Tron Clock at Glasgow Cross, where he addressed large crowds of people. B.T.I. must have been a lively place with Jock Troup, Peter Connelly and W.P. Nicholson numbered among its students! In later years, when Nicholson preached restitution in his gospel campaigns in Belfast, the shipbuilding firm Harland and Woolff had to build sheds to hold the huge amount of stolen goods returned by men who had been converted to Christ.

The larger mission halls of Glasgow used to put on ambitious Christmas programmes, advertised in glossy brochures, featuring special guest preachers and singers. For many of the poor in Glasgow, the brightness and warmth of these meetings counteracted the cold fare facing them at home over the Christmas/New Year period. The wives and children of drunkards dreaded Christmas and Hogmanay, which were harbingers of debt and degradation for many.

I remember reading about a film I thought I would like to see, in the Christmas programme of the Seamen's Chapel in Brown Street. My wife Jean, who was my girl-friend then, agreed to come with me, and we left the comforts of her home to take a tramcar ride into town. We walked briskly along Argyle Street and arrived about five minutes after the meeting had started, to discover that the hall was packed out with Glasgow's poor. We gave away our statutory bag of buns, given out at the door, to two of the lads beside us. The smell was palpable, and grew stronger as the meeting in the warm hall proceeded. We lasted out by passing Jean's perfume-soaked handkerchief back and forward, then staggered thankfully into the cold but fresh air of Glasgow in winter.

The Superintendents' Trio was well-known in Glasgow in the 1950s. John Moore was at the Tent Hall, Andy Stewart at the Seamen's Bethel, and Peter Donald at the Bethany Hall. They all played the concertina (Peter Donald was particularly good), and sang well at special occasions, like Christmas. Bethany Hall has a fine open building seating 1500 people. It was generously gifted to the Glasgow United Evangelistic Association in January 1903 by James S Napier, with the stipulation that his name should not appear in any minute or report as the donor while he was still alive.

Hugh Munro, bank manager with the Clydesdale Bank, and leader at the Foundry Boys Mission in Garngad, was well-loved. He led large summer camp holidays at Pittenweem. Much later, Mr Munro's son Bill and his wife Cathy visited New Zealand. They attended a small church on Sunday, and were welcomed, and brought greetings as Scottish visitors. After the service, a lady said to them how good it was to hear a Glasgow voice, since she was a Glaswegian. They asked her where she came from, and she said they would not know it, but she lived in Royston Road, Garngad, had attended the Foundry Boys' Mission, and had been led to Christ through the ministry of a Mr Munro – Bill's father!. The world is a small place.

George Hood was in charge at Grove Street. He was a fine Christian gentleman, gentle, courteous and kind. Like Lambhill Mission, Grove Street had a Gospel Band led by Willie Carlisle, an ex-miner and champion trombone player. One of the best workers in Grove Street was Johnny McNee, who played the bass in the Band. He used to give up holidays to paint side-rooms in Grove Street Institute. His son David played the euphonium in the Band, and rose through the police ranks to become Sir David, nicknamed 'The Hammer', Metropolitan police chief in London. The Tent Hall also had fine workers like R.C. Brown, a distinguished Christian gentleman who wore stiff, fly-away collars. He spoke in a careful, clipped style and led wonderful Bible classes, astonishing his students with his perfect copperplate handwriting on the chalk-board. George Bell was also a gifted Bible teacher and man of grace. Willie Brown went out preaching the Gospel from the Tent Hall. He was a converted Roman Catholic, who had been a keen boxer in his youth. He had a face that had been lived in, and had several fingers missing on one hand through an accident. Apparently he said to someone when he was dying, 'Next time I see ye, ah'll have a' ma fingers!'

Lambhill Mission didn't have a Pastor. We had visiting preachers each Sunday, some of whom represented Christian work, and missionary societies with Scottish representation, like the Worldwide Evangelisation Crusade, which had a training college in Prince Albert Road, Hyndland, the Faith Mission, the Southern Morocco Mission, the Mission to Mediterranean Garrisons, the Afghan Border Crusade, and so on.

The quality of the preaching and Bible teaching was very uneven. The sincerity of the preachers was obvious, but their giftedness varied. There was Alex Morrison from the Artizans' Hall who had read the

Bible over sixty times and seemed like a walking concordance. There was a small, theatrical man from Renfrew, a fine preacher, whose favourite phrase was 'yea, verily' (the influence of the King James Version of the Bible was obvious with most of them). There was a man from Ayrshire with a very high-pitched voice, whose opening gambit in one Sunday evening Gospel Meeting was: 'The subject I'm going to talk about tonight, dear friends, is HELL. You might think that is a funny thing to talk about; it won't be very funny if you land there...' One preacher attempted a deliberate, dramatic opening at a Gospel Tea Meeting one Saturday. 'Not last night (pregnant pause), but the night before (pregnant pause)' - interruption by small Lambhill boy -'Three wee monkeys came to my door! 'The wee boy was ejected post-haste. I sometimes wonder what became of him. Another preacher was invited every year, although in all the years I heard him, he only had three sermons - Naaman the Leper, the Lost Boy (Luke 15), and the Lost Sheep (Luke 15), where his riveting opening sentence was 'Sheep! Now sheep are a wonderful animal!' After pondering the grammatical anomalies of this, if it came first, you were free to 'perm any one from two' of his remaining sermons as the evening subject. (By the way, Christians were expected to appear at both morning and evening services in those far-off days.) Another of the preachers had difficulties in the sibilant department. His sibilants 's' sounds were lengthy, moisturised and memorable. He informed us one Sunday morning that 'the sheven golden lamp-shtandsh in the Book of the Revelation were really sheven golden candleshticksh' .

There was a strong emphasis on personal Bible study at Lambhill Mission. The Bible Class teacher and the Christian Endeavour leaders were first class. No matter who the preacher was, it was unthinkable to miss a service. The Christian Endeavour Covenant (which was read aloud in public every month) said, 'I will support my church and its services faithfully.' We had to repeat that aloud at the monthly 'Consecration Meeting'.

A lady member of the Mission conducted a Saturday afternoon Bible Club for the boys (there was a separate one held for the girls), where she expounded subjects like the Letter to the Ephesians, and the Apostles Creed, phrase by phrase, with great devotion and expertise. She worked as a cashier at Glasgow's fruit market in Blochairn.

There were loads of opportunities to testify and give brief Gospel messages in open-air meetings, or to present papers on Biblical topics at the Christian Endeavour meetings. C.E. also had a tight committee structure, so that leading a committee and organising agendas and minutes became matters of routine. In these ways, we developed spiritually and practically. Parties, summer tennis, rambles, and camping weekends helped us to develop socially.

CHAPTER EIGHT –
FORGING AHEAD

The choice of a job was vastly different in the 1950s by comparison with today. The question asked was, 'What would you like to be when you leave school?' Glasgow boys with 'Highers' had a fairly wide choice. Although I had university entrance qualifications, after praying and thinking a bit, the idea of earning money, and making use of my maths/ science was attractive. I thought about doing metallurgy with Colvilles Ltd, Scotland's foremost iron and steel manufacturer. A successful interview later, I joined the band of hopefuls, joining the company as a student apprentice Junior Metallurgist.

We started mid-July, looking forward to learning all about the heat treatment, chemical analysis, physical testing, and microscopical examination of iron, steel and their by-products. Before all that, we had a week's introductory course with meals and coffees provided by the Company.

We were warned before viewing some safety at work films that the accident scenes might make us squeamish, but not to worry, just leave the room, and there would be ambulance men in attendance. We were seated in tubular steel chairs with canvas covers, and the room had parquet flooring. The films rolled on, showing surgical operations on injured miners, bricklayers disappearing under an avalanche of fallen bricks, a structural steel-worker trapped by his ring finger on a girder, falling about thirty feet minus the finger, and sundry other gruesome episodes. The ensuing scenes reminded me of the poem 'The Ancient Mariner': 'As thump by thump, a lifeless lump, they fell down one by one'. The afternoon was punctuated with the clatter of metal chairs on parquet floor, and the swift exit of ambulance men with another patient! (I think six lads were carted off).

The wages were a little more than those of full-time milk-boys, but there was a salary structure, and the promise of in-service education and training. The Company employed a full-time Education and Training Officer. We would be allowed to take day release classes at Coatbridge Technical College, pursuing the Higher National

Certificate in Metallurgy. There would be some shift-work involved in our routine jobs, but we would be allowed one day off per week, as long as we passed each stage of the exam - S2 and S3 for the Ordinary National Certificate, and A1 and A2 for the Higher National Certificate. Exam failure meant a repeat year at evening classes, three nights a week, before our day-release studies were restored. In the earlier stages of the course, failure at the evening class stage meant conscription into Her Majesty's forces for two years! Even there the Company cared for us, paying us the difference between our forces wages and the wage we would be earning with Colvilles Ltd.

There was an introductory course for all of us young hopefuls. We attended at the Technical Offices in Brandon Street, Motherwell, next to Dalzell Steel Works. There we had free lunches in the staff canteen, lectures and film shows about the steel industry and industrial safety, and visits to works which were part of the Colvilles combine.

After our initial interview, we had taken a battery of tests set by the Institute of Industrial Psychology, and had been told where we had been allocated. In my case, it was Hallside Steel Works, Newton, beyond Cambuslang, the oldest steelworks in Scotland. From 1881-1890, the total tonnage of Clyde-built vessels made of steel rose from 14% to 96%. David Colville, founder of our Company, had sent his eldest son David to learn the Siemens-Martin (German) method of open-hearth steel production, brought to Scotland under licence at Hallside, which was known as the Steel Company of Scotland works. It was an old, dirty works when I first saw it, with a little village of workers' homes beside it, and, importantly for escape purposes, a railway station which provided a main-line link with Glasgow Central. The works was about to have a new lease of life, producing steel for the Caterpillar Tractor Company which had just set up a factory at Tannochside, Uddingston. Hallside was to have a new metallurgy department.

On our first day at work, the two of us allocated to Hallside were pitch-forked into the practicalities of work, immediately. We had been told to report to the Melting Shop Laboratory at 9 am. There the chief chemist tossed a coin, and I had to shout 'heads' or 'tails'. My colleague John was sent home and told to return to start his backshift (2-10pm), and I was to go home and return for the nightshift (10pm–6am). The first phase of our training, therefore, was chemical analysis, seconded from the metallurgy department.

Hallside's chief metallurgist was really a clerk with attitude, who knew as much about metallurgy as my granny. The chief chemist was a competent, fair-minded Yorkshireman, and the lab staff were a crowd of interesting characters, to say the least. I was about to learn about self-preservation as well as chemical analysis.

I was 'the boy' on the shift with two older men. The head man was a stout, avuncular Lanarkshire man with a moustache, the man who 'got his education at the Cosmo'. His specialties were, firstly, bad-mouthing his mother-in-law, whom he hated with a perfect hatred, secondly, expounding his encyclopaedic knowledge of pornography, and playing chess and golf. Some of the chess was played with my other shift-mate, on a chessboard nailed to the underside of a drawer in the lab, between furnaces 'casting' (emptying out their molten metal and slag). The other shift-mate had been chief chemist at a cement plant, but had had a nervous breakdown.

I'll never forget my first nightshift at Hallside, especially the time when they both settled down to have a sleep on the benches. Before they did that, the shift leader left me with a set of instructions.

'In the room next door, there's an axe and a saw, and some brown paper bags and string. It's the boy's job to get the shift's firewood to take home in the morning. It has to be tightly packed, tied in a circle in even lengths at the bottom of the bag. And watch out for the rats! They're like collie dogs. If you throw bricks at them, they throw them back.'

So here I was on the first night at work, wandering in the darkness, amid the weird shadows and metallic sounds of the steelworks, searching for firewood, and wary of rat attack.

I met most of my other colleagues when I came off nightshift. One of them was the fittest man ever to fail an Army medical, a disgustingly fit young stud who challenged me immediately to an arm-wrestling contest. (He liked to maintain at least a physical sense of superiority in the place.) I was sent with him to sample producer gas. We climbed up steel ladders to the roof of the gas producers, armed with a steel rod, hooked at one end, used for lifting the one-foot diameter cover over the producer, a sausage-shaped glass sampling tube with taps at both ends, and a length of rubber tubing with a rubber bung to fit into the hole, once the cover was removed. It was a task demanding great manual dexterity, and a brave-heart outlook on life, especially as the producer was spitting out very hot tar all the time we were trying to take samples. I persuaded them to concede that they should issue safety goggles for the samplers, on the grounds that I had only one pair of eyes, and they were to last me a lifetime. Some men regarded it as an assault on one's manhood to take safety precautions like wearing hard-hats or 'Totector' shoes with steel under the leather toe-caps, or to wear masks in the foundry as a protection against dust inhalation.

I enjoyed my time in the melting shop lab. I learned the rudiments of what would today be called 'bucket chemistry'. The social interaction was rich, and Friday lunch-times and Sunday breakfasts were special. On the former, someone would carry a mass order from the canteen through the works to the lab, the pile of plates separated with their aluminium collars. On Sunday dayshifts, we used to have a glorious 'fry-up', served on large watch-glasses the size of dinner plates. Tea was, of course, always taken from lab beakers.

When I left the melting shop lab, the chief chemist told me I could come back anytime. He said he respected my Christian stance, and asked me to take a piece of advice with me through life, even although it came from an unbeliever. 'Never close a door behind you, son. Always leave a place or a job in such a way that you could always go back.' I thought that was very kind of him, and I have tried to behave like that.

Back in the metallurgy department, there were other dirty jobs to do! When my time in the melting shop lab was over, and I was back in his section, I felt that my boss gave me a hard time, partly for his own defence against a smart young whippersnapper, and partly because of my Christian testimony. We had a disagreement when I moved a 'nudie' calendar he had put on the wall above my desk, and put it on another wall.

The melting shop were hoping to extend the life of the nozzles which were used to pour the steel from the ladles to the ingot moulds, by tarring them. Guess who got the job of tarring nozzles day after day? Later on, when the exothermic tiles which were ordered to fit into the heads of the ingot moulds didn't fit, guess who was sent to the foundry day after day to file exothermic tiles? My Christian teaching on the need to suffer as a Christian, as well as live as a Christian, stood me in good stead!

For a six-week period, three of us were sent on a time and motion study of a 100-ton open hearth furnace, on three shifts. We were investigating why this furnace was so inefficient, but it gave us close contact with that peculiar creature, the steel melter, which I found interesting. Everyone in the place had a nickname. The head melter on the 'A' furnace was called 'the hangman' because of his constantly miserable facial expression. He could neither read nor write, but could in those days of 'piecework' calculate his wages, or work out the profit on a three-cross double lodged with the bookmaker, to the nearest penny. The bow-legged boss of 'B' furnace was, of course 'Cowboy'. The 'C' chief was known as 'the blink' because of an unfortunate 'tic'. The 'D' chief, whose shift I was following, was known as 'dear oh dear', because he was in the Salvation Army, and when things went wrong on the shift, he said 'dear oh dear' in preference to swearing. The 'E' chief was known as 'Banana Tam' because that was what his wife generally put on his pieces.   One man, too scared to open his piece in public, slipped it under the grill one night, and created a gooey mess because his wife had put 'potty heid' (potted hough) on his piece. There was a wee labourer who became a Christian through the Christian Brethren, and suffered terrible persecution. They cursed him, did everything to embarrass him, spat in his tea, and even hung him up on a hook, trapped by his dungarees. The Brethren offered to get him a better job, and he refused help, because he said he felt like a missionary in darkest Africa! I really admired wee John.

The steel melters earned their money, especially after what was

Herne Bay Court (Guest Speaker) – 1982

called 'a bad bottom', when the molten metal had ripped out the furnace lining. The melters had to shovel dolomite (calcium magnesium sulphate, a grey-white powder) through the open doors of the furnace into the intensely hot furnace lining. They sweated profusely, and their veins stood out like string. 'Dear Oh Dear' had removed his shirt like the rest of them, and when he went to get dressed, someone had stolen his braces! Can you guess what he said? He was left with no visible means of support...

The best tea I ever tasted was during those weeks on the 'D' furnace. It was made in cans placed at the partially opened furnace doors. I guessed from the linings on their cans that it didn't really matter whether they remembered to bring fresh tea. There was enough of a deposit to do the needful.

The melters' card school was a tough educational centre. One of my fellow-investigators was lulled into a false sense of security all week, and then relieved of the contents of his pay envelope on pay night! Gambling was part of daily life for so many. There was a school playing solo whist on the train coming and going to Glasgow Central Station, and during the lunch hour. The morning tea break was spent debating and deciding which horses to bet on each day, to keep the works bookie's runner busy.

I had training breaks from Hallside - three months each at the Research Department, General Metallurgy section in Motherwell, where one of our jobs was to report on a big chest of nails recovered from a Roman camp at Inchtuthil near Perth, and at Clyde Alloy Steel works, Craigneuk, Wishaw, where I learned the secrets of heat treatment and physical testing. I also learned to hold my own in lab fights, where we threw lumps of cotton wool, soaked in whale oil (used for quenching hot steel), at each other.

The chief chemist at Clyde Alloy was very suspicious of a Quantometer machine the Company had bought to do spectrographic analysis. He used to go sidling up to his chemists and ask them to check results the machine had given - all in a whisper, as if the machine could hear what he was saying.

Before the Hallside boss managed to break my temper and wreck my self-confidence, the works was closed for conversion from open-hearth operation to electric arc furnaces, and I was transferred to Clyde Iron Works, Tollcross, Glasgow. The back gate of the works was opposite the Glasgow Corporation Auchenshuggle tram terminus.

Clyde Iron Works had been producing cannon and cannon balls

for the Napoleonic Wars. Some had been found when they were excavating an old well, and were on display. I discovered a Blast Furnace Laboratory full of energetic young men with a tremendous sense of teamwork. Some were of course on shift-work, analysing hot metal coming out of the furnace, before it was taken across the River Clyde to Clydebridge Steel Works to be made into steel, mainly for the construction industry. The blast furnace area was a dangerous place to be. One day, a melter was walking past the slag tap-hole on the blast furnace when it blew out, and he was covered with molten slag. He suffered a high percentage of burning. I was told that molten metal forms globules, but slag sticks to your skin. He lasted three days before he died.

We had minor accidents too. One of my colleagues was talking while reaching behind him for his 600 mls. tea beaker, picked up the wrong beaker, and drank mercuric chloride by mistake. He was rushed to Glasgow's Royal Infirmary to have his stomach contents pumped out. Another fellow dropped bromine liquid into boiling water, which one never ought to do, and was off for six weeks with bromine burns to his face and hands.

The iron works was as replete with characters as the steelworks. One wee, fat electrician claimed to be able to tell by putting his hands around a cable whether it was live or not. His claims were proved wrong when he had a severe electric shock. Our sampler resembled a leprechaun, ideally built for climbing in and out of railway wagons. He was one of the first in his district of Sandyhills to have a television, and he told the following story. Donald, the wee boy who lived in the flat below him, asked if he could get in to watch children's TV, and the sampler reluctantly agreed, but only if Donald promised that he would be quiet and would go away as soon as the programme was finished, so that the sampler and his wife could have their tea. After a few weeks of trouble-free viewing, Donald asked whether he could bring two of his wee pals in. The sampler agreed, and the viewing went on for many weeks, until one day the two wee pals came hesitantly to the door, explained that Donald was 'no' weel', and would it be alright if they still came in. 'Of course, boys,' said the sampler. When the programme was over, the boys lingered at the door until one of them said, 'Will we just give our tuppence to you the night, Mr So-and-So?' Donald seemed set for fame and fortune. The lab labourer responded to an audience, and of course we goaded him into several indiscretions by using the repeated phrase;

'Is that right, Tam?' His best story concerned his greyhound. 'Well, ye see, the trouble with that greyhound was, he wis too clever. He had figured oot where the hare ran, so he used tae jump the fence, run straight across the track, and be waitin' for it comin' roon the corner'.

The old watchman used to come up for a wee blether, and sometimes we had tea together. He regaled me with stories of the First World War. He claimed that when the men in his company had used up all their allocation of ammunition for the day, 'they used tae throw stanes at the Germans'.

The fearful descriptions of the rats in Hallside were excelled in Clyde Iron Works. The rats up near the coke ovens in the by-products plant were like collie dogs! Apparently, rats adapt their diet to suit their environment, and our rats lived on a staple diet of sulphuric acid tar. Their bodies were bloated and their fur was black and sleek. Sometimes, so the story went, when men left out a lot of water for them, they used to drink it - and explode! I had never thought of exploding rats as a hazard in public works. There were always plenty of cats, as well as rats, about the works, and there always seemed to be cat-loving workers who brought them in food and milk. I wasn't too keen on the cats either...

I wasn't up the by-products end much. Many of my fellow-chemists had motorcycles (Matchless 350s were favourite), and during the Suez Crisis, when there were petrol shortages, the boys ran their bikes on nitration benzole from the by-products plant, and settled for de-coking their bikes at very short intervals.

One memorable nightshift (26th June 1959), I joined the number who made a watchman's hut at the coke ovens area of the works seem like the Black Hole of Calcutta, as we crowded round a radio to listen in to the world heavyweight championship fight where Ingemar Johannson knocked out Floyd Paterson, destroying the form book, and providing Sweden with its first-ever world heavyweight champion. These were wonderful years. We sharpened our wits on each other, and played football regularly. One of the lads played for Queens Park, and two played Junior football with Kirkintilloch Rob Roy and Johnston Burgh. Another played ice-hockey with Paisley Pirates. When he had a bad shift, he used to throw pulp (filter paper soaked in water) at the walls. You could assess the state of Dan's nightshift by the amount of pulp adhering to the walls.

Sometimes, coming home from the nightshift, the Auchenshuggle tram put me to sleep and I went past the Central Station and landed up at the Kelvin Hall instead of Possilpark.

I got some interesting analysis to do in the lab, making up the standard solutions, and doing the residual elements analysis each month. As one who was reckoned a good writer, I also got the job of writing up the analysis book for typing each day. When the wee chief chemist died and his assistant got the job, the lab became a sheer delight (not that things were bad under the previous chief). The new boss's primary aim was that the work was done well and that the lab was spotlessly clean (or as spotlessly clean as it could be with all that sinter dust floating about in the atmosphere). When I had Christian meetings, it was possible to swap shifts and there was much 'come and go'. I was in the last group eligible for conscription into Her Majesty's forces. My call-up had been deferred because of the Higher National course, but they decided not to conscript us, so I escaped National Service. I had been looking forward to it, because my Faither and brother had served in the forces. Colvilles were also very kind to their workers. They possibly hoped to inspire loyalty by paying the difference between the Forces' wage and the Company wage into your bank account, so when the boys had served their two-year period of conscription, they came home to a healthy bank balance.

Towards the end of my H.N.C. course, I began to think and pray and plan about the future. When the Iron Works was busy, and all three blast furnaces were going, shiftwork involved running about like a headless chicken, doing analysis of the iron. However, at this period things were in recession and only one furnace was working. If it tapped early on in the nightshift, for example, there was nothing much to do until morning, so I began to take in my Bible and study the call of God to leaders in the past. The account of the call of God to Jeremiah in chapter one of the prophecy convinced me that I should move out of the job I loved, to train for what the church folks called 'full-time Christian service' at home or abroad. I took advice from my Bible Club leader, who gave me information, and arranged for me to meet a Glaswegian former student of London Bible College, which was reckoned to be the best evangelical Christian College in Britain. I applied, and was called to interview on the week I started backshift. In those days, the coach journey from Glasgow to London lasted thirteen and a half hours! Therefore it turned out that I had twenty-seven hours travelling for a fifteen-minute interview, and got back on the Wednesday morning, in time to start my backshift at 3 pm. When my acceptance letter came, I had the problem that I could not have a Scottish Education Department grant because my Scottish Higher passes were reckoned equivalent to GCE 'Ordinary' level passes. I regarded this as a deep insult to Scottish education. I did not have the entrance qualifications for the London University BD degree I hoped to take at London Bible College, and would have to take two GCE Advanced Level subjects with my other College subjects in first year. The first year fees would amount to much more than my savings, so the decision to go to London Bible College was going to involve me in a lot of faith and prayer. I can look back and say in that first year, I had over £650 in gifts. I had a Scottish Education Grant for the remaining three years of my course. They paid my tuition fees, and three instalments of grant at £110 a term.

Working for Colvilles Ltd had been a tremendous apprenticeship in the University of Life. There I had learned lessons of leadership, teamwork and service. I learned how to submit reports and to relate to colleagues and superiors. I had seen the worst aspects of human selfishness, learned awareness and discernment of laziness and incompetence in the work-place. I had learned to work hard without

Baptist Ministers, Jerusalem, Israel – 1981

supervision. I also learned to stand up as a man and a Christian in an occasionally hostile environment, and be an apologist for the Christian position. It was good to take pleasure in a job well done under laboratory conditions, which passed the scrutiny of my bosses. I got the Ordinary National Certificate in 1958, and the Higher National Certificate later with second class passes in Physical Metallurgy, Fuel Technology and Foundry Practice. I resigned as an employee of Colvilles Ltd, and began at London Bible College in September 1960.

CHAPTER NINE –

SERIOUS STUDY

In September 1959, my brother Jim's twelve-year engagement with the Army expired, and instead of signing on for another nine years, as we expected, he came home. This was a surprise. Ma had found life financially difficult pretty soon after Faither's death, once the insurance money ran out. She arranged a house exchange for a flat with a cheaper rent in Hamiltonhill. When Jim came home, in the good providence of God, I was now free to consider studying away from home, since he was around to look after Ma.

Jim hated the first job he got in Civvy Street, labouring in Lewis' department store in Argyle Street. He got a job in the Northern depot of Glasgow Corporation Cleansing Department, in Sawmillfieid Street, near the Round Toll. I was on nightshift on the same week Jim started his first nightshift in his new job. I got home about 9 am, to find him groaning in bed, and learned that he had lasted only half-an-hour on the first shift! It transpired that the group of sadists he was assigned to were known as 'The Flying Squad'. They were paid on a tonnage basis. The amount they earned for the rubbish they put in their lorry each shift was divided by the number of men in the squad. They were therefore dedicated to 'destroy' any new man imposed on them. The rubbish they lifted was emptied or shovelled into large wooden baskets, or 'creels', and they specialised in overloading any new man's creel with bricks, or chunks of tiled fireplaces etc. Jim told me the man before him had lasted ten minutes, and through the grace and favour of the squad and the gaffer, he was to be given another chance! After a few shifts, he demonstrated his prowess to the squad, and thus began a twenty-nine year stint of working for 'the Clennie'. This was to result, after a long spell of street sweeping, and being on the 'gully motor', (which sucked sewage out of the drains), in reaching the dizzy heights of being on the shop motor, where all manner of perquisites, like coffee, tea, cakes, chickens and beer were provided by shopkeepers overjoyed with the service given.

Leaving home to study at London Bible College meant leaving Jean, my wee girl-friend. We had been going out together for two years, a curious blending of opposites - the noisy with the quiet, the bookish with the not-very-bookish, the sporty with the non-sporty, the untidy with the organised, the crowd-lover with the well-nigh claustrophobic, the Corporation school-boy with the fee-paying school-girl. Her parents were Mission Hall people with a strong fundamentalist faith. She was an intelligent, articulate and disciplined person, with a wide range of skills. She was neat and small, and wore glasses. I had a strong urge to protect her and look after her. She was not the slightest bit impressed by any of my achievements. She knew her own mind, and had a fascinating ability to sum up situations and reach decisions almost immediately, decisions which in the vast majority of cases were proved correct. God knew I did not need an 'adoring wife'! Although we had a 'go-slow' policy during my first year at London Bible College, we were married two months after my course ended, and are forty-six years married at the time of this editorial work. Her father worked as a hospital secretary/administrator with the Health Service, at Stobhill, Mearnskirk, and Ruchill Hospitals. He later had to administer Foresthall in Springburn. Her mother had worked in the linen department of Pettigrew and Stephen, in Sauchiehall Street.

Plans to establish London Bible College had been proceeding before World War II, but had to be put in cold storage for a time. The exploratory sub-committee was chaired by Rev W.H. Aldis, and included Rev J.R. Howden, Dr D.M. Lloyd-Jones, Montague Goodman, J. W. Laing (builder), and Douglas Johnson of Inter-Varsity Fellowship. While war was raging, the first evening classes were held in autumn 1943.

The first Principal, appointed after two terms on the full-time teaching staff, was Rev Ernest F. Kevan, a Strict (Calvinistic) Baptist. He was a good academic, a brilliant administrator, a born teacher (specialising in Dogmatic Theology, and later in Homiletics and Pastoral Theology), and a richly-experienced pastor.

He was Principal for nearly twenty years. The College aimed to offer the best of conservative evangelical scholarship to a new generation. The College was also keen to bring the intellectual powers of evangelicals into the market-place, so to speak. It was hoped that there would be an outflow of graduates who would combat charges of obscurantism by achieving academic success in London University examinations, and help to present an evangelical answer to damaging critical conclusions about the Bible.

The 'conservative' part of the description relates to theological conservatism, a desire to retain the best of traditional scholarship's approach to the Bible. The term 'evangelical' denotes four basic characteristics, which have been helpfully delineated by Dr David Bebbington:

1. Biblicism – the centrality, inspiration and authority of the Bible in worship, devotion and study.
2. Conversionism – belief in a decisive personal experience of God's grace in Jesus Christ.
3. Crucocentrism – the Cross of Christ is viewed as a key feature of Christ's life and ministry.
4. Activism – an obligation to practical service and mission as our grateful response to God.

Ernest Kevan's approach to discipline was breathtakingly simple ('If the Holy Spirit called you here, He means you to obey the rules! '). His lecturing style was easy and memorable. He would occasionally say: 'Put your pens down, and listen. You'll remember this!' He was a fine preacher, in great demand, and a brilliant children's speaker, holding huge audiences of children spellbound as a speaker at Scripture Union rallies in Westminster Central Hall. He was married, but had no children of his own. He and his wife used to have three different lady students to tea one afternoon per week.

Mr Kevan (he got his Ph.D for a thesis on the Puritan doctrine of law, towards the end of his life) took the opening meetings in the College chapel, and then stood at the door on the first evening, greeting each student by their Christian name as they left (we are talking about 230 students, and someone who had taken time to memorise their photographs!). That was the last time he addressed us by our Christian names until the evening we left College.

I discovered later that his desk was always cleared by 9am, and that any letters he received were responded to by return post. Of course, he had an excellent secretary, Miss Williamson.

The student body was a mixed group, including French, Dutch, German, Swiss, Greek, Vietnamese, Australian, American and African (I had a Joel and an Amos in my class, and there was a Ghanaian in College who could speak in a broad Glasgow accent, because his teacher back in Ghana was a Church of Scotland missionary). There were people from all of the Christian denominations, so there was ample scope for cut-and-thrust in the theological debate at the meal table and in the Common Room. (a Baptist student once circulated a tract entitled' What the Bible teaches about Infant Baptism', which was blank inside!)

I discovered that there seemed to be a good proportion of the English contingent who had attended public school (in Scotland we would have called them 'private schools'), and a small but vocal Scottish colony, mainly 'tartan-tearers', some of whom were wealthy enough to wear kilt outfits on Sundays. We campaigned successfully to have a copy of 'The Scotsman' included in the newspapers ordered for the Common Room (it replaced one of about six 'Daily Telegraphs'). The College was located at the corner of Marylebone Road and Nottingham Place, across the Marylebone Road from the London Planetarium, and about five minutes walk from Regent's Park. There were three student hostels in Nottingham Place, along from the main College building - Mitchell House for the girls, and Laing House and Aldis House for the boys. I was in Aldis House for my first two years and in 'digs' in Maida Vale for the remaining two years.

There was for me an agonising adjustment to College life in my first year. I felt a great sense of diffidence in the presence of these confident young English people. Making the College first eleven for football, and having some examination success helped me to settle. My allocated room-mate for first year was an ex-classics teacher in a grammar school, an inveterate bachelor it seemed, until he told me near the end of the summer term that he had been going out with one of the girls for most of the year. Bill was also a fan of 'The Archers', an everyday story of country folk, on the radio. He told me this like someone confessing mortal sin. I joined him in listening to the programme at 6.45 each night, although we were breaking College rules (compulsory study Monday to Friday 6 pm-9 pm, and Saturday mornings from 9am-12 noon.) At the time, College rules didn't seem too restrictive, although I have sometimes wondered how red-blooded young adults, in the middle of London, with all that adrenaline pumping round their bodies, were able to keep the rules. Courting, betrothal, and marriage were allowed only with the permission of one's tutor. One of my pals decided to test the system by getting married during the Christmas vacation. He was expelled on the first day of the new term!   Another student I knew posted a note to his girl friend through the letter-box of the girls' hostel: 'My darling Elizabeth, I have given you up for Lent!' The Faculty rule was that any kind of couples should be seen more often apart than together.

During the summer term, the College girls crossing Marylebone Road to go to Regent's Park to play tennis, had to run the gauntlet of wolf-whistles from the office-workers. A new rule was devised which caused an uproar. The girls had to wear raincoats over their tennis dresses! After two weeks, the Faculty recognised how ridiculous the rule was, so the law was repealed.

I had to pray a lot for money during the first year, as my savings would only cover the first half of the first term. Older Christian friends at Lambhill Mission and the church as a whole endorsed my call by giving good support. One man, the afore-mentioned Willie Gillies, gave me £100 cash in an envelope - ten crisp, new ten pound notes! This was the first time I had seen a hundred pounds together in one place...

The teaching staff at LBC were a fine bunch. I enjoyed the painstaking scholarship and gracious approach of Dr Donald Guthrie, my New Testament tutor. Dr Ralph Martin, my Theology tutor, ravished my mind with the range and possibilities of study he presented and modelled. Mr H. Carey Oakley, our Greek and Ancient History tutor, was an elderly, red-faced man with a shock of white hair, and a white walrus moustache. He had been senior Classics master at the City of London School. He was a bachelor who spent his summer holidays walking throughout Europe. His godliness was so apparent that it would have been no surprise to see him zapped through the roof, translated like Enoch, into the immediate presence of God. He must have been well into his seventies when I was his student. He lost his 'cool' only once, to my knowledge. Our Greek grammar book was written by H.P.V. Nunn, and students could buy a 'Key to Nunn', which gave answers to the exercises in the book. Mr Oakley was handing back the homework one day, and said, 'Mr So-and-So, you must resist strenuously the temptation slavishly to copy out Nunn's Key. There are mistakes in it, and I happen to know where they all are!' Leslie Allen, a Cambridge man, was my Hebrew tutor, and has since achieved a fine reputation as an Old Testament expert. Our Philosophy tutor, Rev Dr H D MacDonald, a man from Dublin, provided a kind of cartoon guide to the philosophy of religion, and the history of philosophy, which was immensely helpful when we got down to deal with the highly technical language of the textbooks. He used memorable phrases, like: 'Some of you think your soul is a wee thing hanging inside of you, like an electric light bulb', or 'Karl Barth, now how can I sum him up? He taught that God drills a hole through the top of your head – vertical revelation!'

Saturday evenings were a bit difficult. Although there was excellent available female 'talent' among the LBC girls, I had an arrangement with Jean, and after the first year we were sure that our future lay together. I never asked any girl to go out with me, but enjoyed their company about the place. One girl used to doodle on her lecture notes a drawing of a cat sitting on a wall. She became interested in my room-mate, and the doodle changed to a big cat and a smaller cat on the wall. As their friendship deepened, she doodled a big cat and a smaller cat, with three kittens sitting between them on the wall. She married him, and they had three children, which interested me in the possibilities of 'prophetic doodling'.

If I wasn't involved in College evangelism or College Choir engagements, I used to go for tea with my famous Auntie Nellie (the 'Hallelujah'), and then spend Saturday evenings in London's Classic cinemas, watching films like 'Shane' or' Judgement at Nuremburg', 'Witness for the Prosecution', and so on. Spare-time activities included football training at Regent's Park on Monday afternoons, and playing for the first eleven in inter-Collegiate league matches on Wednesdays. When I was captain of the football team, someone (perhaps a Tottenham Hotspur supporter) chose our new strip – white jerseys, which were very difficult to keep clean. I deliberately sat opposite a lovely sonsy farmer's daughter at the evening meal, and asked whether she knew about my weakness for plump arms. I asked whether she liked getting these arms in a wash-tub, and she said she just loved washing and ironing! Who was I to deprive her of that pleasure?! A big polythene bag, a big packet of washing powder, a Christmas gift token, and she very kindly took a bag of muddy football jerseys for almost the whole season, and returned them, washed, folded, AND IRONED, every week...

In the summer term, I played tennis in Regent's Park on Wednesdays, and enjoyed travelling as a member of the College tennis team for matches with other Colleges. I remember being totally thrashed in the final of the College Tennis tournament.

We had a College Choir led by Rev Owen Thomas, one of our tutors, and I was able to continue the interest in Christian music which was so much part of the life of Lambhill Mission. Our most memorable Saturday engagement as a College Choir was a performance of the whole of Handel's 'Messiah' in Duke Street Baptist Church, Richmond, when Rev John Bird was the minister. It was essential in the College ethos that students took part in the evangelism programme. In my first year, I took part in a team which took weekly services in an old folks' home in Marylebone, called 'Luxborough Lodge', where 1,200 old people were resident. We had a man from an Eastern European country in the team. His English was so rudimentary that at his interview the Faculty were not quite clear about his Christian experience, but gave him the benefit of the doubt and monitored the situation. If you happened to be at this man's table for tea, he would reduce his fellow-students to stunned silence at the expletives he produced at regular intervals. It turned out that he had learned his English in a factory, and thought that swear-words were normal English syntax, to be used for emphasis! Each one of us took a turn to be the team preacher at the old dears' service. I remember this man's talk. He had written it out in a spiral shorthand notebook, and he went on for forty-five minutes on 'The Four Rests of Hebrews Chapter Four'. He had lost his audience very soon after the start of his talk, and after about twenty minutes an old lady shuffled out and came back, wheeling a tea-trolley, and parked it beside him. She started rattling the cups and saucers, while my friend droned on, 'And now, we come to Canaan Rest', etc.

In my second year, I ran an open air meeting in a street market in Kentish Town, opposite the Communist open air meeting. There was much happy banter between ourselves and the Communist open-air leader. During this time I attended Highgate Tabernacle, and heard the splendid preaching of an Ulsterman, Rev Jackie Graham. On Sundays during the first year, I enjoyed the hospitality of the good folks of Fulham Baptist Church, where I taught Sunday School. I helped occasionally by giving a short Gospel address at the food van run by the London Embankment Mission, which operated near Villiers Street, Charing Cross. The homeless ladies and gentlemen were given a mug of tea and two sandwiches. They then had to stand against the wall until they 'got the Gospel', before surging forward for a second helping of tea and sandwiches. The organiser said tersely, 'As far as these folk are concerned, the success of your talk rests on its brevity!"

I conducted an Easter children's mission in Kettering, and was student pastor to Rev Hugh Robinson at Edmonton Baptist Church in my third year.

The football was very enjoyable - four seasons on grass pitches! This was paradise after playing on some ash pitches in Glasgow, where if you fell, it seemed as if you could bleed to death...

Football and examinations were two means of self-expression for me in the early terms. Our 'needle' matches were against Spurgeon's College, in South Norwood, our great rivals. For away games, we would arrive at their College gates to find a Spurgeon's man with a tile hat and claw-hammer coat, and a bell, leading a group of four students similarly dressed at each corner of a coffin they had constructed, with 'LBC RIP' painted on the side. The Spurgeon's College students formed up behind this coffin, and they marched around the football pitch, chanting 'LBC RIP' as the bell tolled. The matches began with prayer in the centre circle, then no quarter was given or received for ninety minutes! I played left-half for LBC (my hero was Dave Mackay, left-half for the great Tottenham Hotspur team of the sixties), and Spurgeon's had a guy called Ted Sampson on the right wing. He was the British Commonwealth quarter-mile champion. If you failed to tackle him immediately, forget it, for he was haring down the wing. In the providence of God, although he was a great runner, he wasn't a very good footballer. (everything's mixed with mercy!).

During my time at LBC, Tottenham Hotspur had one of the finest club sides ever seen in Britain, including the Scots Bill Brown in goal, Dave Mackay, a great attacking left-half (of special interest because that was my position), and a very clever inside forward called John White. There were also the silky skills of the Irishman Danny Blanchflower at right-half, the lung-bursting pace of the Welshman Cliff Jones at outside-left, and the goal-scoring genius of Jimmy Greaves. There was an archetypal bruiser at centre-forward, Bobby Smith, who terrified defenders. I also saw some fine Arsenal games at Highbury, especially a great F.A. cup-tie where Arsenal drew 4-4 with Liverpool, and Ian St John of Liverpool (ex-Motherwell) scored one of the finest headed goals I have seen.

I was fortunate to make the College tennis team, and we enjoyed going around basically the same circuit as the football team.

Because of my sense of inadequacy in Bible knowledge, I did not take up the option open to me after the first year of BD studies of doing the BD Honours course. I concentrated on the College Diploma, where I was one of three in my year who obtained Associate-ship of the London Bible College with Honours. Later on I re-entered the BD exam and up-graded my degree to Honours standard.

Vacations from College put me back on job-hunts back home, because I did not relish spending vacations in London, even although jobs were much easier to obtain there. Each Christmas I worked for the Post Office, spending the first Christmas on letter deliveries in the Parkhead area of Glasgow (some court summons letters, lots of Giros, and one Alsatian dog which mashed up Christmas cards as I put them through the letter-box). The other years I spent sorting parcels in the Waterloo Street office. It so happened that we got our nightshift wages before the last shift of the week, so there were a few out on the final shift who had been quaffing the amber nectar. The foremen were vigilant, and one worker blew his cover by doing a right-turn hand signal as he pushed his hamper on wheels towards the toilet.

One summer I worked as a dish-washer in the Ballachulish Hotel. This was agony, because the weather was foul, and when the staff wanted to say anything they didn't want you to hear, they simply lapsed into the Gaelic. I later worked as a tattie-howker (potato-picker) for one day before obtaining 'promotion' into the yard, stacking hundredweight bags of potatoes three-high all day long. For this torture I earned twenty-six shillings a day instead of the one pound of the tattie-howkers. I could scarcely put my hand out for my money each day! I also worked on a pig farm one summer at Bonnaughton, Bearsden, cleaning the pigsties and feeding the pigs. I pointed out to the farmer one day that there was a boar in a sty with two sows, and asked him whether this could be termed 'pigamy'! After a hard half-shift, the farmhouse breakfast cooked by the farmer's wife was wonderful.

Through London Bible College I was made aware of the precious intellectual gift which God had given me, which I knew from then on had to be regarded as a sacred stewardship. London Bible College stretched my mind, laid the basis for a life-time of study, and provided a great all-round training, linking academic study, practical experience, and world vision. Full-time study accelerated reading speeds and learning rates, and the quality of the students around me sharpened my competitive edge in examinations. When College rules about `lights out' would be broken, I bought a flash-lamp and swotted for a Hebrew exam under the blankets - and passed! C.S. Lewis wrote about `storgia' (affection) and 'philia' (brotherly love) in his book `The Four Loves'. I formed deep friendships at LBC which have stood the test of time. I picked up some skills serving as Meals Steward. This was a bit of a nightmare, because the caterer was very highly strung, and it was difficult to calculate or guess how many students would be in for weekend meals. I was introduced to some new cuisine, for example lukewarm smashed-up sardines on toast at breakfast. I was introduced to parsnips which I had never tasted, and steamed sheep's hearts, muttering darkly that we fed this to dogs in Scotland. The caterer liked to keep us on the move, with rhubarb included in the menu one week, and figs and prunes with carnation milk the other. I had never tasted figs, and enjoyed a good double helping at lunch-time one day. One of my fellow-students inquired gently whether I was involved in the Inter-Collegiate five-mile run that afternoon. I avoided major embarrassment by running the best race of my life that day. I think I was twelfth out of 65 entrants.

I also served on the Student House Committee as Prayer Secretary. Being in London, I was able to go and hear the legendary Dr D. Martyn Lloyd-Jones at Westminster Chapel. My room-mate in our digs at Maida Vale in our fourth year had become a Christian through attending Dr Lloyd-Jones' Friday evening Bible Study. The subject the evening he was converted had been Romans 3 verse 25. My friend Bob was later called to serve God in the Christian ministry, took his `O' levels and ` A ' levels, and did a four-year course at London Bible College. During the final term of the final year, Bob went back to the Friday evening Bible Class. The 'wee doctor' had reached Romans chapter 8 - it took him six years to deal with five chapters.

Dr Martyn Lloyd-Jones was one of the outstanding preachers of the twentieth century. He was small, bald, unprepossessing, muted in his dress. Sitting in the pulpit in his Geneva preaching gown, you would have thought that someone had left this small man there by mistake - until he got to his feet. He had left a distinguished career as a Harley Street physician to become a preacher, pitch-forked after years of obscurity in the Welsh valleys into mainstream ministry in the Westminster Chapel pulpit in London, near Buckingham Palace.. He spoke with authority. By the time I reached London, the Chapel was always well-filled. I felt that the Doctor generally preached more freely in the evenings than in the mornings. During my limited period of attendance, he was dealing with Christian warfare from Ephesians 6 in the mornings, and in the evenings the Wisdom of God in the early chapters of 1 Corinthians. Attending Westminster

Chapel could be a lengthy experience. The evening service often lasted two hours. The main prayer often lasted 20-25 minutes. His words were clipped, conversational and attention-catching at the beginning. His preaching seemed to me to be like a plane taking off. He would start off slowly, and then get into full flight. He would often 'clear the ground' by explaining in detail what any given text did NOT say before tackling its positive teaching. He rarely used illustrations outside of Scripture. He illustrated the New Testament from the Old Testament, using his illustrative method and story-telling abilities as means of teaching Old Testament truth. We seemed to sing 'Jesus shall reign' to the tune 'Truro' a lot, and the pipe organ at full blast with the full-throated singing of a huge congregation made you think the whole place was going into orbit. When you hit the cold night air, you felt you could float home!

The other big preacher in the city at that time was John Stott, Rector of All Souls, Langham Place. I attended several of his monthly guest services. He had a beautiful, 'posh' English voice, and preached on well-known Biblical passages with great freshness, simplicity, clarity and power. His after-service question times were a revelation. He invited folk to write questions on a piece of paper. He collected them in and shuffled the pack before giving Alpha plus answers 'on the hoof.'

In November 1962, Jean and I got engaged whilst I was home for half-term. I went before the Ministerial Recognition Committee of the Baptist Union of Scotland, and was accepted for ministry in Scotland, without further training, although I would have to pass Baptist Union exams in Baptist History and Principles.

I left LBC in June 1964, having gained my ALBC (Honours) and the BD degree. On August 15 1964, Jean and I were married in Lambhill Evangelistic Mission, where we had both come to know the Lord.

CHAPTER TEN –

PREACHING AND TEACHING

During the final term of my final year in London I went back to Clyde Iron Works blast furnace lab to see the lads, and let them know I was finishing the course. I had been accepted for Baptist ministry by the Recognition Committee of the Baptist Union of Scotland. The chief chemist at Clyde Iron asked about my plans, and offered me a job, which I took on a weekly pay with a week's notice in case I got a call to a church. I had to devise a method for a new kind of analysis and train a youngster to do it, so that when I left, he could take it on. The 'boy', Andy, is now a Church of Scotland minister in Ayrshire. It was good to don the lab-coat again and fit into normal life and work patterns. I was allowed time off, while Jean and I went on honeymoon to Portrush.

By the end of the year, I was called to Buckhaven Baptist Church as minister. Buckhaven/Methil was a run-down mining area. Buckhaven had a lovely bay. It had been a holiday resort earlier this century, but the sand was gradually covered with pit washings from the Firth of Forth, so the beach was mainly black shale. Mining had brought more wealth to the area, with higher wages, but it was environmentally damaging. The pollution of the water virtually ended inshore fishing, and wrecked a lovely sandy bay where there had been a good tourist trade, mainly from Glasgow holiday-makers. There was an air of decadence about the place. We were to live in a three-bedroomed, semi-detached manse opposite the bowling green. There was a large walled back-garden. The church was spotlessly clean. It had a sloping floor, and fine acoustics. Dr Kevan came up from LBC for the Ordination and Induction services. His recent heart attack meant he had to come by plane, and have a downstairs room in the manse. At the Welcome Social I tried to be careful to thank everyone for everything they had done - decorating the manse, filling the larder, even putting coal in the coal-shed. At the end of the service old Davie, the godly treasurer, came up. 'The coal-man will be for his money through the week.' 'Back down to earth' for the new minister!

I occasionally feel pangs of remorse for what that poor congregation had to suffer from a young guy just out of College, bursting to share his unique world-view and recently acquired erudition with ordinary Fife folk living on the edge of survival. I now read my Buckhaven sermons (I have kept my notes) - and blush. We must have done something right, for when we left in September 1967 the church was usually full on Sunday mornings, and we had ninety-two members.

Baby Finlay arrived in September 1965. He was born in Craigtoun Maternity Hospital, St Andrews, so I was able to use what was known as 'the Happy Pappy bus' to visit Jean and Finlay.

The Buckhaven manse seemed very cold. We used to scrape the frost off the inside of the windows some mornings. We had to dress Finlay in woollies to put him to bed. When Jean's relatives visited us, we were told to order a ton of coal and send them the bill! They also gave us our first television set, a free-standing cabinet with double doors. While on the subject of consumer durables, I passed my driving test and we bought our first car at Buckhaven. It was a black Standard 10, ten years old, which leaked like a sieve, and cost us £75. When the big-end bearing needed replacing, there was no way in the world we could raise the £25 to pay for it, so we sold it for £7-50 for scrap, and got a cash refund on the road tax disc. You would never think in those days of going to the bank manager to ask for a loan. We gave a lot of hospitality at Buckhaven, had a baby and ran a car, but were never in debt. The Baptist Union of Scotland minimum stipend was £625 per annum. If married couples were blessed with fecundity, there were increments of £12 per annum per child, up to a maximum of three, and thereafter you were on your own...

We had some fine people and some good workers at Buckhaven, but the gap between my idealistic expectations and what I perceived was the congregation's 'one-man ministry' outlook, where success and failure were perceived as my success and failure, was too wide. Christians I knew confirmed my teaching gift. After Rev Andrew MacBeath, Principal of the Bible Training Institute, visited our home, I applied to be Old Testament and Hebrew lecturer at the Bible Training Institute, in Bothwell Street, at the heart of Glasgow. After interview I was appointed. We expected to be living on the premises, but were offered a fine, three-bedroomed semi-detached house in Bishopbriggs. We would pay the local rates, and a nominal rent, and I would travel into town for lectures.

'What are you doin' here, son?', was my greeting from Mrs Reid,

College caterer, when I rang the side doorbell of the Bible Training Institute in Bothwell Street. 'You're a day early - the students come tomorrow.' I introduced myself as the new member of staff, and we were off on a new bridge-building project. On my second day I was hailed by Dennis Bullitt, who had served in the US Navy for twenty years: 'Hi, kid, could you help me carry this trunk in?' I helped him, introduced myself to him, and he said: 'You'll soon get to know me; I'm the dumbest student at the BTI'.

The massive tri-partite structure which occupied the site in Bothwell Street, between Blythswood Street and West Campbell Street, took twenty years to build. The central part was built as the Christian Institute in 1878-79, as a direct result of the mission services conducted by the American evangelist D.L. Moody in 1874, in a huge tent erected on Glasgow Green. The architect John McLeod drew his inspiration from the Reformation, and designed a building in German Renaissance style. Statues of John Knox and William Tyndale were placed above the entrance, with carved heads of other Reformers decorating the front of the building. The cost was enormous - over £12,000, with a further £45,000 required for the two wings added later. The West Wing contained a restaurant, and bedroom accommodation for 189 people for the YMCA., and the East Wing contained premises for the Bible Training Institute. Work on the wings started in 1895 and ended in 1898. R.A. Bryden, the architect, followed the style of the original building, and added towers at each end. The chemicals manufacturer Lord Overtoun and his sister dug deep to pay the bills. In my time there were white marble statues of these two worthies in the BTI entrance area, and students with a greater sense of humour than their sense of history, used to add their names to the list of those requiring blood tests.

When our student numbers outgrew the BTI accommodation (e.g. we had 169 students one year), lots of our men were 'farmed out' to sleep in the YMCA. In my time also, the YMCA was the venue for our city-wide Christian Endeavour parties. The whole area provided a focus in the city centre for evangelical work, and the loss was incalculable when the whole building was demolished in 1980.

The BTI was built primarily to provide education for converts of the Moody mission who had only basic education, to prepare themselves for full-time Christian service, for example, in city mission work. For decades, BTI was the only residential college in Britain which offered single study bedrooms. It must have been the last word in modernity when it opened. The laundry area, near the top of the building, had an amazing system for drying clothes. Students could hang their washing over the metal poles which joined two upright wooden panels, and push the panels into an area where pipes from the heating system dried it in double-quick time.

Discipline was fairly strict. The floor presidents were issued with whistles, which they used to announce quiet times, lights out and so on. The male and female residential sides of the building were totally segregated, with the girls' side of the College in charge of the matron, a redoubtable ex-missionary.

In the 1960s, missionary societies required candidates to do Bible training, and some specified BTI for preparation. In addition, the Torchbearers' Fellowship, based on Capernwray Hall, sent Continental students for the two-year course. We had high quality young people from the Netherlands, Germany, Austria and Switzerland. There was always a strong group from Ulster.

The skills of students varied enormously. In the main, stepped lecture hall, you could have a doctor doing a one-year course before going to Thailand with Overseas Missionary Fellowship sitting next to a lad who had been digging ditches for a living the week before coming to College. I was given a class to teach for London University's GCE 'Ordinary' Level in English. This was for students who had lost out on formal education. I also had to take Old Testament lectures for the basic College diploma, the London University Certificate of Proficiency in Religious Knowledge (CRK), and the London Diploma in Theology (Dip.Th.). I was told that Hebrew was a Cinderella subject, where I should teach the alphabet, and how to look up words in lexicons. On the first day of my first year, a student just down from Cambridge University, who had completed his Tripos a year early, and had taken Hebrew and Engineering as interest subjects, asked to do Old Testament Hebrew as his special option for the Diploma in Theology! I took him on, and started a beginners' Hebrew class, presenting candidates each year I was there.

The students were an interesting bunch. One student was so pleased with his girl-friend's gift of a knitted cardigan with leather buttons, that he wore it constantly. One day he decided to wash it, so he put it in the washing machine with very hot water, and lots of soap powder. It came out like stiff felt, small enough to fit a doll. He lost his girl-friend, and wasted his cardigan. He never married.

On Wednesday afternoons I joined the students for football

at Bellahouston Park, and on Wednesday evenings we had a 'floor fellowship' group from College in our home. We had joined Springburn Baptist Church, and I was a deacon there as well as being out preaching regularly.

In October 1968, our second child, Janet, was born in Stobhill Hospital. It was the College Prayer Day, which ended with a Praise Meeting, and I was preaching on the text from Isaiah 26:3: 'Thou wilt keep him in perfect peace whose mind is stayed on Thee.' Jean and Janet were fine, and she grew up to delight us. Finlay was three, was able to understand what was going on, and gave his wee sister a great welcome.

While in Buckhaven, I had registered for the London University BA General degree, but hadn't done any work for it prior to December 1969, yet Jean encouraged me to take the final examinations in June 1970. My old history teacher at Possil School loaned me about fifteen good history books, and I got my relatives to join Glasgow Public Libraries and give me their tickets. The little library at Milton was excellent, providing the 'Pelican Guide to English Literature', and Winston Churchill's 'History of the English-Speaking Peoples', which formed the framework for the English and History sections of my studies (my third subject was Theology, where I chose as many Greek set texts as possible). Woodside Library had the Cambridge Modern European History series, and the Mitchell Library were willing to tell me which district libraries had any books I was hunting for. I was so grateful to God for His help. I studied only enough to pass the exam, but the exams were a test of organisation as well as comprehension. I had nine three-hour papers to take in three weeks. I had studied for six months from 5 am until 11.30 pm, with time off for work and church each day, and spent most of the Easter break studying alongside the dubious characters in Springburn Library.

I had extraordinary help from the Lord regarding one of my English papers. On the Friday afternoon prior to taking the exam on Monday, I realised two things: I had to write for one hour on the 1645 edition of John Milton's poems, and secondly, that I hadn't even read one of these poems, let alone any critical comment on them. I said a wee prayer on the bus, and got off to have a look at Bishopbriggs Library. I found a book to suit me there, and discovered after writing steadily for an hour on the Monday that the author whose quotes and comments I had used was a world authority on Milton, E.M. Tillyard, Fellow of Jesus College, Cambridge.

I suppose I got my degree from Glasgow Public Libraries! I wrote a letter of appreciation to the Library service at the twenty-fifth anniversary of Milton Library. In the final analysis, my degree cost me no more than £50, and was as valid as that of any full-time student who had spent hundreds, or even thousands of pounds. London University had a failure rate of roughly 50% in those days.

Ma died in Ruchill Hospital, as Faither had done. It was September 1971. She was what we call in Glasgow 'the creaking gate', and had outlived Faither by fifteen years.

One day in 1972, I was running up West Campbell Street to catch a bus at Buchanan Street bus station when I was halted by a terrific pain in my chest. I stopped, took it easy for the remainder of my journey, and took to thinking on the bus home to Bishopbriggs. Supposing I had dropped dead. I could trust God, but could I trust BTI to look after Jean and the kids? Was it right to expect them to do that?

I concluded that it was my responsibility to take action. I had made plenty of sacrifices for other people; perhaps it was time to make sacrifices for the benefit of Jean and Finlay and Janet. The medical tests gave me the all clear.

I applied to Jordanhill College of Education, and was accepted for graduate teacher training, offering History as Main Subject I, and Religious Education as Main Subject 2. The five years at BTI had been excellent. I loved teaching, and learned to produce under pressure. I tried to find answers to the key question 'What is a good teacher?' My approach was that the good teacher's task is not to obscure, but to simplify what is complex. A good teacher is there to impart the joy of discovery, not to excite the students' wonder at the cleverness of the teacher.

The good teacher is there to organise as well as to simplify the body of knowledge he is teaching. The good teacher's task is to visualise, to give what is abstract concrete expression, to give it legs, so to speak, to make truth visual as well as viable. An old Arab proverb says, 'He is the best teacher who can turn the ear into an eye.' My knowledge of Hebrew, and English, improved tremendously by having to teach it. Through lecturing at BTI, we formed friendships with students which have gone on through our lives.

God had been so good to us in our married life. The BA degree had been further evidence of His Fatherly goodness. In 1972, we saw a fresh evidence of His goodness in the provision of our own

London Bible College First XI – 1963

home! We had been looking around and wondering what to do, because we knew that giving up at BTI meant giving up the house in Bishopbriggs. After tea-time, on the day I resigned from BTI, my next-door neighbour, Bill, came in and told us they had had an offer for a house in Dumbreck officially accepted. And would we like to buy their house, because they would like us to have it! That night, someone else phoned and told us to go to their insurance broker, who would fix us up with a mortgage. After a few days of feverish activity, everything was in order. When the removal time came, we got a few friends round, and moved into the other half of the semi-detached (much to the amazement of some of our neighbours). We were to spend another thirteen years living in that street.

CHAPTER ELEVEN –

CHANGING THE FOCUS

In the months after leaving BTI, I had two agonising transitions to make – from lecturer to labourer, and from labourer to student at Jordanhill College of Education.

Jim put in a good word for his wee brother, and I got one of the student places allocated each summer by Glasgow Corporation Cleansing Department. There I found myself in the anonymity of the Sawmillfield Street depot of the Cleansing Department, with a group of tough, half-asleep men, answering to our names after the hand-bell was rung and the register was opened.

The assistant boss, nicknamed 'Booboo', was a bumptious wee man who said everything twice, for example, 'That's a brush, no' a feather duster, that's a brush, no' a feather duster.' I once put on a serious face, and asked him if he would do me a favour. 'What is it, what is it?' he said. I explained that I was only there for the summer, but would he allow me to ring the hand-bell one morning? 'Ye need tae be in here a long time before ye get ringin' that bell, ye need tae be in here a long time before ye get ringin' that bell.'

The Yogi of the Northern depot had forgotten to organise putting down weed-killer on the kerbstones and there were weeds sprouting up all over the district, causing bother in wet weather by choking the drains. I was issued with a long steel tool, with an oval ring at one end as the handle, and a steel triangular plate at the other end for removing the weeds. When I had dug the weeds out, I brushed them into tidy piles and the lorry came and lifted them. Simple.

One day in Ellesmere Street, Possilpark, I was surrounded by a group of boys, and the following conversation ensued:

'Whit are ye daein', mister?'

'What do you think I'm doing, son?'

'Ah think you're biffin' oot the weeds.'

'It may look like that, son. (Pause, and voice drops and goes into sinister mode). Actually, I'm a Russian spy and I'm drawing up plans of the drains and sewers in this area. When the Revolution comes,

Janet's Dedication Service, December 1968

we are going to flood the district with poison gas, and you'll all waken up dead.' (stunned silence).

'Ye'll never get away wi' it. Ma da's a polis...'

Another time, a child asked me what I was doing, I said: 'Digging for gold'

'Whit'll ye dae if ye find any, mister?'

'Chuck this job right away' said I.

Apart from providing endless entertainment, that summer's work paid for our lounge carpet.

Jean's parents came in to help us for the Jordanhill year. They looked after Finlay and Janet while I was at college, and Jean, a medical secretary, worked full-time in the hospital. At Christmas I got a job in McManus' 'Man's Shop', in Balmore Road, Possilpark, round the corner from Saracen Cross. The gents' outfitters was located underneath the pawn-shop I used to frequent as a child! The McManus brothers were kind to me and I sold a lot of stuff. I got lots of good questions and comments. The lady shoppers got so frantic just before Christmas and New Year, that you could have sold them anything. I heard gems like:

'Hiv ye goat (do you have) a tie fur ma man? He's a seventeen neck.'

'Hiv ye goat a perr (pair) o' long drawers for a short man?'

'Hiv ye goat a bunnet fur ma man? He's goat a big heid, the same as yours.'

And on Hogmanay: 'Ah don't know whit ah'm daein' buyin' a shurt fur him. He'll jist slabber beer aw doon it.'

My memories of Jordanhill College of Education are mixed. I seem to have spent lunch hours in the vast canteen, wearing my overcoat, and eating my dinner from a tray, feeling like a prisoner-of-war in transit to Buchenwald.

The History department staff were very good. I was told in advance that the Religious Education principal gave evangelicals a hard time. I had to devise a coping strategy for this. Believing, with Erwin Rommel, that the best method of defence is attack, I found that my 'Your scholarship's out-of-date' defence served me well, and we parted with mutual respect, and in the twelve years of teaching which followed, Jordanhill sent me thirty-five students for teaching practice. My first teaching practice in history was in a suburban school with good kids, who got belted far too much, and where there was a poor sense of teamwork among the staff. My second teaching practice in Religious Education was diverted from the original plan, because the R.E. teacher had a nervous breakdown! I was sent instead to Smithycroft Secondary School, a 1,000-pupil comprehensive next door to Barlinnie Prison. (They built the wall to keep the children out, rather than the prisoners in, it was said). The staff at Jordanhill were apologetic about the Smithycroft situation. The elderly man who taught R.E. had just been there for a month or two, and I would have to 'take things as I found them'.

The morning I walked in the front door at Smithycroft, before I had seen a pupil or met a member of staff, I knew that was the place for me. At the end of my teaching practice, the Head Teacher offered me a post, provided my Glasgow Corporation interview was all right. I would do a half timetable in History, and half in Religious Education, in session 1973-74.

I left Jordanhill with the Secondary Teacher Certificate with merit, and the Higher Diploma in Religious Education – and went back to the Cleansing Department for the summer vacation before starting at Smithycroft.

For two weeks, I was nightshift on the side-loader, collecting heavy items like beds, mattresses and washing machines from the back-courts of Possilpark. The rest of my nightshift was spent sweeping the main streets of Maryhill. Glasgow is amazingly alive at night! I witnessed the single parents' pram races in Raeberry Street at midnight. After tea-break, I swept St George's Road to Charing Cross, and Sauchiehall Street from Charing Cross to the precinct. One of the interesting features to me was the illuminated Bible with its magnetic marker, in the window at the Findlay Memorial Tabernacle in Maryhill Road. I rarely passed it through the night when there was not someone reading it.

Early on in my nightshift, I had gathered my sweepings together, and asked one of the men what to do with it. He told me to throw it into the hedge, and I would get it back tomorrow night, and never be out of work. I said: 'Is this the Cleansing department, or the Dirtying department?'

The second half of the second summer was spent on day-shift as a street sweeper in Maryhill. I used Nansen Street for a social experiment. It is a fine, short street with lovely sandstone tenements and wally (tiled) closes, but the street was full of broken glass. The children from a local school were guilty of smashing their glass bottles after buying soft drinks from the shop mid-way down the street. On my first day, I decided to sweep the whole street from end to end, not simply the gutters. I found that a group of children used to gather around every time I went into the street. After a few days, a ground floor window opened and a woman hung out over her window sill, and addressed me thus: 'Hey, mister, are you a poof'?' (Glasgow invective for a homosexual).

'No, I'm a happily married man with two children. Why do you ask that?'

'When the last Clenny man came, the weans ran away, but they're aw roon (all around) you.'

'Well, that's because I talk to them. The adults in this street just shout orders at them. I ask them how many fingers they have, or what colour their jersey is, or what they want to be when they grow up. Is that alright?'

'Aye, that's fine.'

Every day after that, her window opened and she handed me out a Mars Bar and a can of Irn Bru.

We made it through the first year after BTI, managing to keep up the mortgage payments. My grant, with allowances, was slightly more than the BTI salary, and my wages were a help.

I finished work with the Cleansing Department, and after a short break, it was 'Smithycroft, here I come'.

I am grateful to God for the leadership and encouragement of the two BTI Principals I worked with, Revd Andrew MacBeath, and his successor, Revd Dr Geoffrey Grogan.

Before I left BTI one of my colleagues said he thought I had achieved a good measure of self-training, and wondered what contribution Jordanhill College would make to someone he regarded as 'a born teacher'. I found the Jordanhill experience helpful and confirmatory. It was especially helpful in two ways. Firstly, it improved my questioning techniques, and highlighted the importance of questioning in learning and teaching. I had noticed in the Gospels the skilful use of questions by Jesus, the Master Teacher. Secondly, it helped to highlight the importance of means and ends in teaching. Aims and objectives have to be set in advance of the teaching process, and objectives should be defined behaviourally as far as possible, ie, what will the student be able to do as a result of learning this lesson?

The confirmatory aspects of the Jordanhill experience were also two-fold. Firstly, I confirmed that I could transfer from purely theological disciplines to others, and from adults to children at the receiving end. Secondly, the result of a verbal I.Q. test set by the Psychology Department confirmed an ability to tackle any verbally-orientated task.

Despite my initial misgivings at the first teaching practice, the guidance of God had once again become a reality in our lives.

CHAPTER TWELVE –

AT THE CHALK FACE

My own experiences as a pupil had been so helpful that a main element in my thinking was a great desire to pay back something to a new generation of Glasgow school-children. The Labour Government's educational philosophy had set out the comprehensive ideal in education, but in many areas things were far from ideal.

The Reformation in Scotland was a popular movement, rather than a royal imposition, as it was in England. John Knox had been a key figure, although many people are surprised to learn that he was present for only six years at the vital period. His plan was to fund parish schooling from the confiscation of Roman Catholic wealth. The population would become literate, and part of the package was that the clever boys from any parish could have a University education, no matter how poor they were, funded by the State. Although the Lords of the Congregation thwarted Knox's plan, even the truncated scheme put Scotland in the vanguard of European education. Scotland became famous for a good, broad-based education. The idea behind the comprehensive system was not simply to save money, but to concentrate resources on a wide front, which children could have available within their own community. The comprehensive school would have an important role in social engineering, eliminating the damaging social stigma associated with screening children into the Junior Secondary schools.

Smithycroft was a good example of a comprehensive school, because its catchment area was so disparate in the kinds of children who attended the school. Children came from the very best type of Glasgow Council housing, in Carntyne and Riddrie, from Blackhill, which at that time was rated as the worst housing area in Europe, and everything in between. We also had the Barlinnie Prison officers' children. There is no necessary connection between deprivation and bad social behaviour, and teachers, like everyone else, have to guard against labelling and stereotyping. We had some excellent kids from the worst catchment areas, and some very difficult pupils from prison officers' families, since prison officers seemed sometimes to transplant the prison regime into their homes. We also became what was termed a 'magnet school', attracting more than a hundred children from local Roman Catholic schools, mainly for reasons of safety. One or two of these schools were noted for bullying and violence. Roman Catholic parents were willing to submit to our non-denominational regimen, including religious assemblies and R.E. classes, as long as they felt that their children were secure. Our Head Teacher, Robert Lamont, an ex-Classics Principal Teacher, compared them to the slave population in the Roman Empire. The Roman Senate decided not to issue uniforms to slaves, lest they find how many of them there were, and rise up in revolt, like Spartacus! The presence of so many Roman Catholic children in the school also helped keep up the responsibility payment, but it probably exacerbated the Rangers/Celtic rivalry, as active in our school as it was in Glasgow generally. To illustrate how strong the loyalties were, one parent included the middle names 'Kai Johansson' when naming his child, who was unfortunate enough to be born on the day of the Scottish Cup Final, in which Rangers defeated Celtic by one goal, scored by their big Danish defender.

1970 – BTT Outing to Arran.
Finlay on left, Janet on the right.

There were strenuous, and, on the whole, successful efforts to enforce the wearing of school uniform. The Head and a doughty lady Assistant Head policed the entrance hall each morning, able to spot anyone who was wildly out of the dress code. Jordanhill students wearing jeans, and teachers who came without a tie were not exempt from quiet comment and command.

The school building was beautiful. It had been designed by what was known in Glasgow as the 'ARSE' Department (Architecture and Related Services'). It was apparently based on an American hospital design, a bit like a banjo, with a circular main building, with a link corridor to the technical and physical education block, which included a Youth Wing and a swimming pool. In the centre of the circular main section was a lovely, well-finished circular assembly hall. At Christmas dances, this was a godsend to me, who could not dance round corners!

A 'golden staircase' rising from the entrance hall was an eye-catching centre-piece.

The circular building led to all kinds of problems. One day, wee Billy, a third form character, shouted in the English principal's open classroom door: 'Aul' So-and-So's a part-time wrestler!', and promptly legged it round the corridor. Although the English principal was a lady of generous proportions, she set off in pursuit, and when she caught wee Billy, she led him by the ear back to her classroom, and spanked him in front of her class, much to their amusement. (She would of course be taken to court nowadays).

A parent once phoned the Head to complain that Mr So-and-So had belted his son. The Head promised to investigate and phone him back.

'Mr So-and-So, as you know, the school building is circular, and pupil movement is in a clockwise direction. Mr So-and So is in charge of corridor discipline for the ground floor. Your son David was travelling in an anti-clockwise direction, and was properly given two of the belt.'

'But Mr Lamont, David left at Christmas, and was back to school for a reference for a job.'

Across the playground we had a fine annexe building, which cost as much as the main building (£750,000) by the time it was finished. The large hall in the youth wing was in use most evenings for the Youth Club, as Smithycroft was a community school. Thanks to the herculean efforts of the Head, teaching staff, janitors and cleaners, the building was in tremendous order, virtually graffiti-free.

Unfortunately, the flat-roofed areas were constantly needing repair. What about the staff? During my first week, the Head's name was mentioned, and I innocently asked what the Head was like, and back came a reply replete with that instant reaction and disarming frankness of Glasgow's children: 'He's a bloody German tank, sir.'

The R.E. scene was a difficult one. The old gent, who had been there only a short time, was barely surviving. I realised after my second day at teaching practice that I was on my own in the matter of discipline.

R.E. in Scotland was at long last making progress, in the wake of the Miller Report which had recommended a career structure in the subject, with full-time professional teachers. Some areas had appointed Advisers in Religious Education. R.E. could not yet be offered as Main Subject I at Colleges of Education. After my first year at Smithycroft, I was offered a full timetable in R.E., and after second year, the post of Principal Teacher was advertised. I applied and went to be interviewed on the leet, and got the post. At the end of my twelve years there, I was at the top of the salary scale, as an Honours graduate with a responsibility payment for a 1,000 - pupil school.

The R.E. pendulum swung during my time, from having to teach World Religions as of equal value with Christianity, to a later, and in my opinion, a more sensible view that Christianity should be a major part of the R.E. programme, with R.E. part of the core curriculum offered in Scottish schools. Pupils could also opt to do the subject at '0' grade and 'Higher' level. I worked hard with other Glasgow teachers on curriculum development panels to provide lesson material for teachers coming in to do R.E. The Strathclyde Report, thanks, I believe, to Roman Catholic influence, was responsible for a stronger emphasis on Christianity in our teaching programmes.

There was a tremendous esprit de corps amongst the staff. It seemed that the Head attracted people who in general felt comfortable in the ethos he created, without necessarily agreeing in detail with his approach. There were some pretty strong characters there - they were no bunch of sycophants! His leadership style was definitely that of the benevolent dictator. We were almost like being on a war footing, like those old World War II movies: 'we're all in this together, chaps!'

One evening I had a telephone call from someone who had been offered a post teaching mathematics at Smithycroft, and was told to contact me for information about the maths department. I told him that the maths area was the quietest in the school, because the Principal would tolerate only the scrape of pencils on paper as the loudest noise made by pupils in his classrooms. The assistant principal in general didn't talk to adults. He only talked to children, and only in class. The teacher in the classroom next to him was a lady of riper years whose son was a lorry driver. She had lorry driver's mirrors screwed on to the sides of her chalkboard, so that she could keep an eye on the children while she wrote on the board! The teacher in the next classroom was a hard-drinking Partick

Herne Bay Court

Thistle supporter who without warning could drop his jacket partly down his back to do his brilliant impression of a chicken. Finally, at that time the end classroom was occupied by an American lady who was half Red Indian, here for a year's exchange. Apart from that, I told him, the maths department is perfectly normal. He came, and stayed for three years, before heading off to train as a Church of Scotland minister.

There were single-sex and mixed staff-rooms. The men's staff-room in the main building was the smokers' paradise, with a card school

BIBLE TRAINING INSTITUTE
1971

Bible Training Institute 1971

(solo whist) going on at lunchtime in all weathers. Some of us started to play badminton at lunchtime, and do 'The Scotsman' crossword each day between games. The game and the shower freshened us up for the afternoon's activities, and our numbers grew. The sporting and social life of the staff was very active. We had football and badminton teams and we played against other school and college teams. There were also football matches against the pupils, which were well-attended. We took up jogging, and ran half-marathon and marathon races. A number of us ran in the first Glasgow Marathon in 1983.

Every school develops its own traditions. In places like Eton and Harrow, these have persisted for generations. The staff tradition at Smithycroft on Sports Day was for the Principal Home Economics teacher to bedeck her room with memorabilia of the Royal Family (she was a fervent admirer), and to organise tea and strawberry tarts for the staff. The pupil tradition was that the lone parents from years past would bring their babies in their prams to line them up, socialise and watch the races.

Before the angst surrounding teachers' strikes cut a swathe through the profession's goodwill, out-of-school activities flourished. We had over thirty different clubs and sports activities, and the school minibus was in great demand. It was rather like the time of Joseph in the Bible. In the 'years of plenty' we had stocked up, with metal cabinets full of hill-walking gear, and a room full of ski equipment, which we were able to use in the 'lean years' which came later. For the most nominal cost, the poorest children in the school could be kitted out with boots, gaiters, waterproofs, day-bag, and woolly hat. We had football, rugby, volleyball and netball teams. There was canoeing and skiing, war-gaming, chess and a swimming club. I ran the Scripture Union group on Thursdays at lunch-time. During the summer, I led a canvas camp for Scripture Union, for 75 boys, at Scoughall near North Berwick, with up to 15 of my own pupils attending. The Thursday group was attended by about thirty children. We met at 12 noon and had our packed lunch, and then our S.U. meeting was held from 12.30 pm until 1 pm. The school dining-room alternated each week between boys being on first lunch, then girls. Those who attended S.U. were allowed to have first lunch on presenting a note which I signed. The most popular item on the lunch-time menu was pies, chips and beans. I was a bit quizzical, although pleased, to see some unusual characters attending S.U., until the matter was resolved one day as two boys left the room with my signed note, and I overheard one say to the other, 'Aye, ye'll get pie, chips an' beans the day, Alex.'

Jesus had people who followed him for the loaves. In my case, it was the pie, chips and beans.

The S.U. camp site at Scoughall, North Berwick, was granted (for

26 years!) to S.U. by the farmer, on the basis that he might need the field next year, so we were not allowed to put up any buildings. Sanitary arrangements were adequate if primitive, and I was toilet attendant of the dry lavatories for about 100 people. On the first night of camp one year, a Smithycroft boy came up to me at the far end of the field, and asked: 'Where dae ye dae the toilet in this place, Mr Mitchell?'

I pointed airily to the plastic drainpipe nailed to the fence. 'If it's a number one, son, you do it in there.' Then I pointed to the line of canvas-covered cubicles. 'If it's a number two, you do it in there.' A look of utter consternation came over his face at his first brush with S.U. camp bureaucracy. 'Whit dae ye dae if it's number seven? Ah'm tent number seven.'

While we are on the camp theme, one of my tent leaders came to me one year and asked what to do about his boys, who were playing

Four Generations – Jessie Maclean, Jeanie Findlay (her mother), Jean Mitchell (her daughter), Finlay Mitchell (her grandson)

with a hedgehog, because he had heard that a hedgehog was full of fleas.

'You've nothing to worry about, Geordie,' said I, 'because animal fleas won't go on to a human being.'

'They will, if you comb your hair with them!' Geordie replied.

We crept silently to the area behind his tent, to find his boys in that total solemnity which accompanies scientific discovery, sitting in a circle, passing the hedgehog to see what it felt like as a hairbrush.

I had the privilege during the later period of my twelve years there, to take Smithycroft pupils to Iona Abbey Youth Camp, and other places. At the end of my first year in the school, I had just returned home from our church Sunday School picnic, when the phone rang. The Deputy Head at Smithycroft asked me to come up to the school and help comfort the parents. The coach returning from Iona with our pupils in it had collided with a Land Rover, and had plunged down a railway embankment. Three pupils and a student teacher, a married man with four children, had been killed. One of the pupils died being comforted by the Head, who had gone up for the last few days of camp. We stayed with the parents until the last of the children involved were released from Vale of Leven Hospital. A school is a microcosm of society. As a member of the staff team, I had to learn, like Ezekiel, to 'sit where they sit', and share with pupils and staff as

Bible Training Institute Lecture Hall – 1967

113

a fellow human being. It was a reminder that a school is a microcosm of life in its tragedies as well as its joys.

I was asked once to accompany a third year group on a week at an outdoor centre in the Highlands. Glasgow Corporation had bought this place, refurbished it beautifully, and had put in a team of instructors. The warden of the place had applied for the post in protest at the school where he taught in Edinburgh becoming comprehensive. Instead, he found himself, by one of life's strange ironies, receiving kids from some of the poorest areas of Glasgow, every week -including us!

He got the pupils together for the introductory keynote speech, which went something like this:

'I don't care if your bodies rot at the bottom of Loch So-and-So, but if you want to swim (it was January and sub-zero by the way), you have to ask permission. I don't care if you rot your lungs with the foul weed tobacco, but there is no smoking in this centre. Also, you will receive none of your beloved Glasgow 'ginger' (soft drinks) here, because you're not going to litter our lovely countryside with broken glass. Finally, DO NOT FEED MY DOG!'

During that January week, things went from bad to worse. His punishment for making any noise after 10 pm was to have children out in their pyjamas for half-an-hour, cleaning boots in the sub-zero temperature of the quadrangle. When we were returning home after a day of foul weather on the hill, he had the minibus stopped, and sent a boy out in a howling gale to bring back a sweetie paper he was supposed to have dropped half a mile up the road. The last act in the drama occurred when he reluctantly agreed to the pleadings of the girls to put a TV set in the lounge, so that they could watch 'Top of the Pops' on the Thursday evening. In the middle of the programme, the Bay City Rollers, who were in their heyday at that time, came on. Our girls' screams were interrupted by the warden rushing in, unplugging the TV set, and carrying it off! There were terrible linguistic repercussions from my pupils.

Throughout the week, it was salutary to meet the warden's enormously fat dog, and to see the kids on several occasions, quietly and deliberately feeding the beast with a Mars Bar. It was their only way to strike back at the warden.

So much for the Smithycroft building, the staff, and the extra-curricular activities. What were the pupils like?

We begin with a pupil's perception revealed in a question asked

when a teacher's salary cheque was sent up from the office.
'What's that, sir?'
'It's my salary cheque.' 'Oh, where do you work?'
The Glasgow children specialise in quick-response one-liners, which was very disconcerting for some of the Christian speakers I brought into school. I remember one guest who was supposed to be taking my class for the day in exchange for some favour he had done us. He was ready to leave by the morning interval, mainly because of the directness of the questioning he was receiving.

One day I was reading the script supplied with a filmstrip on the Life of Isaiah the Prophet: 'And there flew unto me one of the seraphim, having in his hands a live coal taken with tongs from off the altar. And he said to me, "Lo! This has touched your lips, and your sins are taken away, and your guilt purged.'

Back came the instant addition to the text from the school bully at the back of the class, 'An' yer mooth's aw burnt.'

The pupils were, in general, lazy readers, and would sometimes read the first part of a word, and guess the rest. The modern textbooks use the form 'Yahweh' instead of the old form 'Jehovah'. A boy read one day: 'You shall worship Yamaha your God, and him only shall you serve.' A further example was: 'Now John the Bastard was walking by the banks of the Jordan.' Teacher's murmured correction: 'John the Baptist, son.' Pupil response: 'Sorry, sir, John the Baptist.. .' We then proceeded as normal. No one had laughed. The rest of the class had thought his original form was correct.

Sometimes, senior pupils got the story wrong. One pupil was describing the movements of the Ark of the Covenant, and the misfortunes it had caused to the Philistines who captured it. The Philistine god Dagon had fallen on his face before it, and smashed into pieces. The pupil wrote: 'This wasn't the end of the trouble for the Philistines. There was an epidemic of haemorrhoids in the Philistine camp.'

One of the Jordanhill College students, who was coming for teaching practice, came on a preliminary visit one Friday afternoon, when I had a class of third-year, non-certificate girls. They couldn't pronounce his name, so he was christened 'Mr Diarrhoea' for his time with us. My questioning exposed their appalling ignorance of things African (half the class thought Scotland was bigger than Africa). At the end of my interrogation, I said, 'Well, now, I've asked you a lot of questions. Have you any questions you would like to ask Mr So-and So?'

A hand shot up at the back of the class, and Jeannie asked: 'Dae yeez werr claes wherr you cumfae?'

'I beg your pardon?' said the cultured African gentleman.

'She's asking what kind of clothing you wear where you come from, Mr So-and-So,' (Mitchell escapes another embarrassing situation). We had some very clever and talented children. It is always salutary to face a class, and think that there are children there who might be cleverer than the teacher.

Some people denied that Smithycroft was a genuine comprehensive, preferring to describe it as a thinly-disguised Senior Secondary, because it was not a totally mixed-ability school. A broad-banding method was used, with mixed-ability within the band. Class sizes were preferentially weighted to suit the less able, slower learners. In third and fourth years, the children came to R.E. in their English sections. Although I was never off sick, the strength of ten horses was required for the daily round. Initially, I had one period of SI-SIV per week for R.E. which meant a turnover of around 700 different pupils per week. To get them in, settled, and overcome the customer resistance to being made to work, especially in my first year, was quite tiring. We needed all that fitness training in badminton and football.

Later on, the Ordinary Grade in R.E. came in, and we had a section doing that. One year, I had a girl who had passed Higher Latin, and wanted to do '0' Grade Greek in a year. I managed two periods per week, and the Principal Classics teacher next door managed one, and we took her, successfully, through the course.

There were some difficult children. Three former pupils were in for murder during my time there. Others were in prison for possession of arms and ammunition with intent to kill, and many of the current pupils were found guilty of minor crimes, especially car theft. One boy who stole a Corsair 2000E and was eventually apprehended after a police chase, said to the arresting officer, 'Ye cannae dae (charge) me this time, ah'm no' on a public highway.' He was driving in and out of the tombstones in the local cemetery at the time.

Another boy who had behaved badly was put in the auxiliaries' room until help came from higher up. He spent the time while he was waiting filling his mouth from a tube of Gestetner duplicating fluid, and spitting it round the walls.

Some pupils were dreadful under-achievers, and some achieved things far beyond normal expectations. Motivation is a key factor in education. One boy who was very keen on becoming a nurse, wanted three 'Highers' - and got them, against all odds. Other very promising children became University 'drop-outs'.

The children were often hard on one another. I remember saying to a boy whose reading was poor, and his writing deplorable, 'Would you like to try and draw this, son? Are you good at drawing?' His class-mate responded, 'He's nae good at nothin', sir.'

One pupil was a speech therapist's nightmare, with dreadful deficiencies in the 'l', 'r' and 's' departments. Glasgow boys named 'Robert' are often known as 'Rab'. In his case he was known as 'Lab', and his class-mates used to goad him into saying 'shiensh labolatoly'. One day he came into my classroom and said, 'Hey, shir, gonnygeezalenniapenshil' (please may I borrow a pencil). My response was 'Who do you think I am, Robert - Santa Claus?' Instantaneous reply, 'Shame build azh Shantaclauzh, shir.'

One pupil in an English exercise wrote the word 'chookiedinbra', which was recognisable only from its context 'the Queen and the...'

One day after a class had left the room, I discovered a desk-top covered with lewd and libidinous drawings. I deduced who the culprit was, and wondered how he could have managed all that art-work in one period without being detected. I resolved to watch him carefully the following week. He was drawing on a rubber, and stamping the desk with it! I pounced half-way through the period, and hit him hard. Although I had caught and punished him, we remained good friends, and he even asked to come away with the Scripture Union group for their weekend camp at Troon. I saw him returning from our outing to town with a suspicious brown paper parcel, which I managed to smuggle out of the boys' dorm. When I opened it, sure enough, there were six cans of beer. Later on, he spoke to me: Sir, someone has stolen something from me.'

'Oh, I'm sorry, David! tell me what's missing.'

'Well sir, to thank you for taking us away for the weekend, I bought you six cans of Heineken lager, and they've gone missing.'

'I'll tell you what, David. You tell me the name of the man who sold them to you, and I'll have him charged for selling booze to an under-age person.' Panic.

Although I never had a dull day as a teacher, I felt that I had 'paid my dues' to society after twelve years. I seriously attempted throughout the period to act professionally as a teacher, but to live as a Christian in my work environment. I found that staff members came to me for counsel. I encouraged keen S.U. children to cast in their lot with the local Church of Scotland, and eventually there was a Youth Fellowship with over twenty of my pupils involved in it as confessing Christians. Teaching was a stressful occupation, and R.E. teachers came for help, and I found myself being an encourager at teachers' conferences at Seamill.

My pastor, Brunton Scott, preached the sort of sermon on the first Sunday of January 1984 which galvanises people into action. I felt the call of God back into the Baptist ministry after eighteen years. My name was circulated around the Scottish Baptist churches, and I went as pastor to Portobello, part-time in 1984, and full-time in 1985. Being a school-teacher for twelve years confirmed for me the viability of the Christian life in what was basically a secular society, and in situations of stress daily. Wearing one's heart on one's sleeve was not only unprofessional, but highly dangerous. The children exploited

George with Jack Spiers, Portobello Baptist Church Secretary – Atholl Centre, Pitlochry

to the full anything that had even a whiff of weakness. They kept pushing for the boundaries, and if they found none, the teacher at the other end was not only exposed but destroyed. We had one young Honours graduate who had spent five years preparing to teach, and lasted one term, before leaving to become a hall porter in a hotel. He was a shy lad, away from home in Glasgow, and the senior girls embarrassed him into leaving. They asked him out for dates, and told him how handsome he was, and so on. Another teacher who had a first year class for registration and guidance, and two periods a week in his own subject, inherited them for an additional five periods of English, when there was a shortage there. They drove him over the edge. He was absent for weeks, and it later transpired that he had been leaving home each morning, and returning home each evening as if he had been at school. He told me he used to sit in George Square, or the Central Station, or the Mitchell Library, wondering how he was going to face that class of twelve-year-olds! It didn't pay to be soft! Another teacher left to go to Sardinia to write a novel, but was actually living on the dole in a basement flat in Byres Road. Fortunately, he returned to teaching later. I was once asked to address a group which ministers to people with alcohol problems, and was surprised to find one of my colleagues in the group – for help. I know that kids can drive teachers to strong drink, to insanity, or to have suicidal tendencies. I used to say with great conviction, that I never had a dull day in twelve years of teaching.

One day after school, a lady R.E. teacher from another school arrived at my classroom door to tell me that she had been spat on by a pupil that day. When she reported it to her Head Teacher, he told her he was sorry, there was nothing he could do; that was the image her subject had in the school. I knew her career was doomed. She retired early, hurt, soon afterwards.

Jesus said that His followers were to be like salt and light. In everyday work, the Christian is, in a sense, to be rubbed into the meat, to have an impact and an influence, without compromising professional status. Sometimes situations cried out for compassion and intervention. An unkempt boy, cruelly nicknamed 'Wurzel' by his classmates, was wearing thin sandshoes with holes in the soles in the dead of winter. I spoke quietly to him at the end of class, and offered him a pair of Doc Marten boots our son Finlay had outgrown (they were the right size). He came back by arrangement after school next day. The boots had plenty of wear left, and I had given them an

Army-type polish. He wore them for one day, and next time I saw him, he was back to the holey sandshoes. I learned later his father probably sold the boots for the price of a pint of lager.

As I said earlier, the Christian R.E. teacher has special problems relating his faith to his job. He may believe that Christianity is a subversive counter-culture, but he has to be careful not to abuse his position, especially in our multi-cultural, multi-faith society. There was a Kingdom Hall of Jehovah's Witnesses opposite our school gates, and we had a number of children from JW families who were abstracted by their parents from assemblies, but never from my R.E. classes. I used to wonder why, but concluded that my sympathetic treatment and defence of these children as a persecuted minority might have something to do with it. My conversations with the JW pupils revealed that they did not fully share their parents' convictions and beliefs.

I found it possible to fulfil professional obligations without going mad with Christian frustration! Christians are good at talking about 'incarnational Christianity', and I think being a Christian R.E. teacher is one way of giving it legs. I have to say that, Miller Report notwithstanding, some of my colleagues were in a bad way, and I met some pathetic pill-poppers and boozers at R.E. conferences. I have found that going to these conferences as a teacher and as a minister is rather like visiting the hospital - you always meet folk in a worse state than yourself.

I had enjoyed being a Christian presence and influence in Smithycroft Secondary School. Some parents were kind enough to thank me for being there. My colleagues thought I was committing financial suicide (the Portobello stipend was about £6,600). We sold our 'semi' in Bishopbriggs, and moved to Portobello in June 1985.

CHAPTER THIRTEEN – ACROSS THE POND

In the goodness of God, we have been able to travel. Our favourite area in Scotland since teenage years is the Moray Firth coast, especially the small towns of Cullen and Findochty. We were involved in what was known as 'The Endeavourers' Mission' for several years, when about a hundred of us went to Cullen during the Glasgow Fair Fortnight to conduct a children's mission, involving a morning meeting on the sands, sports, fancy dress parades, 'visitors-versus-locals' football matches, evening hymn-singing at the harbour, and so on. We virtually took over the town for two weeks! Later on Jean and I were able to visit France, Italy and Greece, and I was privileged to lead pilgrimage tours to Israel.

In 1986, we had an American Partnership Team in Portobello, and in 1987 I paid my first of five visits to the US of A. I visited all our team, and preached in their home churches in Georgia - in Athens, and Atlanta and Dublin. I was interested to see the Americans on their own patch. After all, they had passed my brother Jim back through the lines when he escaped from prison camp in Czechoslovakia during World War II. Our team had come at their own expense to minister in our church. The British have been greatly influenced by the USA. through cinema and television, and blue jeans and McDonalds have a universally pervasive influence.

Nations and Christians tend to produce stereotypes of each other. The British stereotype of American Christianity is first of all, that it is shallow and superficial, 'three thousand miles wide and half an inch deep'. Secondly, the British tend to have a superior attitude towards theological training and academic standards, and you can almost hear the mutters about 'Mickey Mouse' degrees. As far as I am concerned, the stereotype is off-target and inaccurate in both respects. My experiences of church life, although brief and limited (Georgia, Virginia and Illinois), were at close quarters, and brought me into contact with some of the finest, most committed and spiritual Christians I have ever met. I had hospitality from a quiet and gracious millionaire who, (so others told me), supported totally at least twenty overseas missionaries, lived very simply, and drove a twenty-year-old car (a beautiful Oldsmobile). He was a Professor of Mathematics who had not missed a University of Georgia football game (American style) since 1928! He took 18 of us to lunch after I preached in his church, and in good mathematical mode, checked each item in the bill before paying. He used to charter a liner, pay a preacher, and invite Christians to bring their unconverted friends on Gospel cruises in the Caribbean.

American Christians are very committed to evangelism and mission, home and overseas, and 'put their money where their mouth is' in financial support. The Southern Baptists have a huge missionary budget. They were very generous to me during my visits to the Sunday School Board offices in Nashville, and the Mission Board offices in Atlanta.

The Americans were interested in the Scottish expository style of preaching, and also by the homiletic structure of our sermons. The American exposition I heard tended to be verse-by-verse, unstructured, and heavily anecdotal. I have heard only a few American preachers, so I cannot say whether they are representative.

With reference to academic standards, I had the advantage of London Bible College/London University courses as a basis of comparison with the Trinity Theological Seminary, Indiana, with whom I did Ph.D. studies. In my estimation, in some areas (such as philosophy and Old Testament archaeology) the Trinity material was absolutely excellent. I was disappointed in only one area (New Testament), but Dr Ralph Martin and Dr Donald Guthrie were world-class, a hard act to follow.

I saw my first live American football game in Georgia, when the University of Georgia played Louisiana State University. LSU achieved victory in the last few minutes of the game, watched by an 82,000-strong crowd. It was good to be in the October sunshine, and to sense the family atmosphere of the 'tail-gaters', cooking their steaks on the back of their pick-up trucks in what was obviously an all-day outing.

One of my hostesses offered me extra coffee at breakfast, but despite my refusal, she put down a jug on the table, so I dutifully 'topped up' my coffee. Her husband picked up the jug and poured it over his waffles! I sat back, trying to adopt an urbane expression, drinking a cup of (mainly) maple syrup.

I asked another hostess, Louise, why a street in Athens, Georgia was named 'Plum Nelly Road', and she replied 'because it's plumb outa town, and neahly in the country'.

The churches I was in were very busy, and geared for growth. Prince Avenue Baptist Church, Athens, had a large ministry team of trained specialists, their own school, radio station, wonderful games facilities, a fleet of buses, a marvellous robed choir and two wonderful lady musicians playing the piano and organ. The evening congregation numbered several hundred, and the majority were young people (Athens is the home of the University of Georgia, and had 26,000 students in 1987). When the dynamic Pastor Bill gave the invitation after my sermon, about thirty-five people came forward and were taken into side-rooms for counselling. They re-appeared later to tell the folks what God had been saying to them about their lives and service.

I returned to the USA in 1990 with a team for a 'Here's Hope' mission in Clairmont Hills Baptist Church in Alexandria, Virginia, where we had a great welcome and wonderful hospitality. On my first morning, I went into a local shop and asked for a map. The lad was very helpful, even when he returned with a floor-mop, and I explained that I was looking for a geographical map!

Our daughter Janet married Curtis, an American, in 1995, and we were able to visit their homes in Palatine and Elgin, Illinois, and worship in local Baptist and Nazarene churches. We thank God for our American brothers and sisters.

My other trip 'across the pond' was to South America. In May 1998, I visited my pal David, who is a missionary in Sao Paulo, where he is involved in church-planting in the favelas (shanty-towns).

I first met David at my brother Jim's removal from Musselburgh to Kirkintilloch. We became instant and constant friends, soul-mates, and together with Ivor the Irishman, a psychiatric nurse (every Baptist minister should have a psychiatric nurse for a friend), we formed a hilarious troika of common Christian interest and close loyalty. (Jean refers to them as my 'playmates'.) David had learned to live by his wits in the Garscube Road area of Glasgow (if you've got teeth there, you're a 'softie'!). He was the boy who went for the milk at school, so that the teacher could have a few minutes of peace. His education was extremely rudimentary, but he became a time-served mechanic with a razor-sharp brain, his own garage business, a flashy car, a fine home, a wife and two children, a good set of golf-clubs and a raging thirst for what is called in Glasgow 'the fa' doon watter' (whisky - when you drink it, you fall down). David's boozing and street-wise philosophies brought him into conflict with the 'powers that be', and he found himself minus car, home, family, and business. He came to Kirkintilloch, and after a dramatic conversion to Christ, he began to rebuild his life and prepare for work in Brazil with his second wife, Cath. I became the Professor Higgins to his Eliza Dolittle in the courses set for him by the Baptist Missionary Society. One day we had an argument when I said 'Jesus wept' was an English sentence, and David disagreed because it was too short! He passed the Cambridge Certificate in Religious Studies. He and Cath were missionaries long before they hit Brazil. Their council house in Kirkintilloch seemed always to be thronged with battered wives, teenagers on drugs or drink, and people in need of food or shelter, or a shoulder to cry on. When they reached Brazil, David proved to be the fastest learner of Portuguese they had seen, learned from the people rather than the grammar book. His street wisdom from the Garscube Road was very useful in Sao Paulo. They built the first church from wooden packing-cases procured from the Volkswagen factory. Soon Cath was running mother-and-baby clinics (she is a trained nurse and midwife), and English classes, and the Brazilian Baptists were encouraged into co-operation. The help of richer churches was sought out. By the time Ivor and I arrived, David was Association Secretary for the Brazilian Baptists (one of the areas he is responsible for has two-and-a-half-million people living in it).

Sao Paulo is wall-to-wall people. The inner city has about 11,000,000, and Greater Sao Paulo has about 26,000,000. It is one of the most dangerous places on earth. The number one cause of death is road accident. They drive like maniacs: I spent a fair amount of time cowering in the back seat, singing 'In the sweet by and by'. The number two cause of death isn't heart attack, strokes or cancer, but gunshot. We saw evidence of a strong, armed, police presence. When I went to the market to buy Brazil strips for the Inverness youngsters, someone stubbed their cigarette out on my arm so that I would remove my hand from my pocket, the easier to pick it! It didn't work – Scots would rather have a burned arm than an emptied wallet.

The favelas are built on spare or unclaimed land, or rubbish dumps. Mafioso-type organisations or religious groups move in, and exploit the squatters by demanding rent, imposing 'protection money', or selling them housing materials. The families begin with the simplest structures of wood and sacking etc, and the rough rule is that if they have up-graded to bricks and mortar, if the city authorities move in, they have to be re-housed.

David showed us a deserted favela site which had been occupied by over two thousand families. It looked like a World War I battlefield. The authorities came one day, and gave the people an hour to clear out their stuff before it was bulldozed and set on fire. David stood weeping with hundreds of families as the bulldozers moved in, seeing everything they owned destroyed before their eyes, chilled within with the thought that all their money and effort was wasted,

Janet's Graduation Ball with Finlay

and they would have to start again from scratch.

To gain access to the first favela home we visited, we walked across a makeshift bridge over a burn of urine running down the hillside, and went into a spotlessly clean Christian home where Mum, Dad and four children were living in an area about twenty feet square. Some of these folk were professional people whose homes had been repossessed by the bank, and they were working their way back up the ladder. The dad in this first home had had his own home, car and business, but his father had forged his signature on vital documents and had hopped off to Rio with a young woman. Osiel came home to discover he was homeless, car-less and jobless. He became a Christian, and has since bought a piece of ground, and with the help of the believers, and a strong personal faith in Christ, is building a new home.

The people are amazingly hard-working and resilient. After our first visit to the favela, Ivor and I stood crying like babies. David said, 'What are you crying for? That was a good one I showed you. If I'd taken you to a bad one, you'd get shot!' We saw mothers in cardboard boxes in the busy city areas, with their children begging from the cars which stopped at traffic lights. If children are troublesome to motorists, car drivers are perfectly free to shoot them, and drive away without fear of prosecution.

People play football all day long. There was a concrete pitch near one of the homes we visited, with available time split into twenty minute intervals, with new teams coming on each period. No wonder the Brazilians are world champions at football.

I lectured at a Baptist College with 125 students (over sixty came to an optional evening lecture), and I saw their library, which was smaller than my own at home, and half of the books were in English. I was able to hand over to the College Principal $400 which a Highland Christian had given me before I left for 'some good cause'. He would buy a few books for the library. We were also able to phone home and raise enough money (£750) to put the roof on a favela church. Planning permission? – forget it! The materials were ordered on the Tuesday, delivered on Friday, and in place the following Monday. We saw how the Baptist Association had started, under David's leadership, an 'Adopt to Educate' scheme funded by the richer churches. Children have to be able to read to join the State system of education. Parents have either to teach their children to read, or pay to send them to pre-school. Favela parents can do neither. David had seventy-five children in small groups, each led by a qualified Christian nursery teacher. Otherwise, they would be condemned to be illiterate. We saw a clothing store, a book store, and a food store for the poor in an 80,000-population favela area (Heliopolis). We worshipped in growing churches full of joyful, zealous people, attracting lots of young people. We watched a candidate for the ministry being 'grilled' for three and a half hours by Association ministers. They expected him to give answers on the spot, from his Bible as necessary, to a wide range of questions on Christian doctrine and ethics. I felt our students in Scotland would find this rather severe.

The holiday components of our visit included going round a few of the modern shopping malls which favela kids will never see, and a visit to the golf club (membership mainly Korean and German business people), where it costs $15,000 to join and $7,000 a year to play. We also went to Santos with its beach, and saw the stadium where Pele used to play, which was for me a kind of pilgrimage.

It is obvious that we could not take in all that was going on in two weeks. Our love and concern for David and Cath as representative missionaries increased greatly. We will never forget the welcome of the Brazilian Christians, or these hard-working people and their lovely children. Sadly, David's marriage collapsed under the strain. His son has married a Brazilian, and they have children, and are doing a great work among the street children of Sao Paulo.

Portobello has Latin American connections. In the skirmishes between the British and the Spanish navies in the Spanish Main, a certain Captain Jenkins of the Royal Navy lost his ear, and his devoted seamen pickled it in a bottle, and brought it to Parliament in London. The 'War of Jenkins' Ear', was later known as 'The War of the Spanish Succession'. In 1739, Admiral Edward Vernon of the Royal Navy sacked the town of Puertobello ('the beautiful port') in Panama, and in 1742, one of his seamen built a house in the outskirts of Edinburgh, and called it 'The Portobello Hut'. A settlement developed around it, and the house remained intact until 1851. The new Town Hall was built there, but space was limited, and the new Town Hall was built in 1878 on the site of the present police station. The old Portobello Town Hall was built on the site of the Portobello Hut in 1862. Designed by David Bryce, complete with griffon gargoyles and gothic clock. The building became the Star Cinema, and the building was later bought by the Baptist Church. Rev D.Merrick Walker, R.N. was appointed by the War Office to minister to troops in five centres near Portobello, and after World War I he accepted the full-time pastorate of Portobello Baptist Church, which was strategically situated in the centre of town, in Portobello High Street. The wooden church hall was brought from Gretna about 1920, was erected behind the church and was readily accessible from the main street.

By the Victorian era, the town produced bricks, pottery, lead, paper, soap and mustard, and nearby Joppa was famous for salt production. Portobello Sands were used to exercise the Edinburgh Light Horse, and Walter Scott, a quarter-master with them before he achieved world fame as author of the Waverley Novels, was kicked by a horse in 1802 and had to rest in Portobello!

Sir Harry Lauder was a native of Portobello. The power station provided heat for the famous outdoor swimming pool, and Fred Barney, channel-swimmer extraordinaire, lived and trained there.

Portobello was a great tourist attraction. The indoor swimming pool had Turkish baths attached. Many Glaswegians slept on the beach during the Glasgow Fair fortnight, I was told. On a sunny Sunday, there can be around 25,000 day visitors. The beach and prom are lovely!

Jean and I got involved with this amazing place in 1984, and we moved there full-time in 1985.

Finlay was doing his Electrical and Electronic engineering course at Strathclyde University, and Janet started her Home Economics degree course at the Queen Margaret College in Clermiston.

Portobello somehow retained its identity as a community. Glaswegian friends used to ask me what was the difference between Glasgow and Edinburgh. I told them I used to travel by bus from Waverley Station to Portobello on Sunday mornings. I looked round the lower deck of the bus one Sunday morning, and counted six ladies wearing fur coats. You could travel for a hundred years on Glasgow buses, and you'd never see six fur coats! Another example of difference came when our neighbours went on holiday and the wife asked whether I would pay the window-cleaner while they were away. I agreed of course, and she counted out one pound fifty into my paw. I said: 'Is it not three pounds for the window-cleaner?' She replied: 'Oh, we just get the fronts done'…It has been said that Glasgow people tend to be wasteful, and Edinburgh people tend to be careful. I found the Portobello Baptists very generous and responsive when there was work to be done. They raised over £20,000 for a roof repair, and transformed the wooden hall behind the church, to say nothing of refurbishing their beautiful manse before we came. The manse was a fine Georgian terrace house in Joppa, built in 1907, with a Dumfries sandstone facing at the front door. An estate agent would have said that it had seven commodious rooms, with high ceilings and tasteful cornices. Finlay's bedroom walls needed eleven rolls of wallpaper. When we removed the flush panelling from the doors, we uncovered lovely yellow pine doors. There were two lovely wooden fire surrounds, one of them in a bedroom, which the hard-working church team moved to the front lounge. The church shared the cost of carpeting with us, and we had the best carpeting that Springburn could sell! They sent away the doors and one fire surround to be 'stripped and dipped' and installed gas central heating. I spent some time, money, and a whole summer clearing and re-planning the beautiful garden area, which was below street level, accessed by a stairway down from the kitchen door. A far cry from Lochside cottage, I hear you say! When the church eventually sold it, they got a handsome price, to say the least.

The church hall had big ugly heating pipes and radiators that didn't work, so we removed them, and won about a foot in width each side. We hired a sander, and removed the years of grime from the fine timber floor, put on about five coats of varnish, and improved the lighting. An unemployed painter and decorator redecorated the whole place, and we were nearly ready for action. The hall had been regularly used for an elderly ladies' meeting on Thursday afternoons. The finished programme included a Monday Centre for Alzheimer sufferers, to give respite for their carers, with massive help from Social Work Department, an Alcoholics Anonymous group on Tuesdays, a group for special needs adults on Wednesdays, Women's Own on Thursday afternoons as usual, a busy coffee morning meeting point and sale of goods on Friday and youth club on Saturdays. We had space beside the church in the main street which was rented and refurbished by the Citizens' Advice Bureau. The pub next door shared our roof and so were liable for part of the roof repair. The pub owners Dryboroughs Brewery had been taken over by Alloa Breweries, and I had an interesting meeting with the Estates Manager where I was trying to persuade him to give us the pub, so that we could turn it into Edinburgh's first non-alcoholic pub! I explained that we would be happy to acknowledge and 'pub-licise' the Brewery's kindness in this matter The punch-line in the conversation was his expressed opinion: 'It isn't commercially viable, sir, to give away your property.' You can't win them all...Edinburgh people are not mean, they're just careful.

The Edinburgh people were wonderfully kind when the world-famous American evangelist Billy Graham came to Britain by Live-Link, satellite TV broadcasts. When I heard about the possibility, I wanted to do something about it. I thought that Portobello Town Hall would be a good venue for the meetings. I had a judicious conjecture of 600 people a night for the week of meetings, and this would mean a budget figure of £6000, and the Billy Graham organisation wanted £600 (10% of budget) up front. I went to the Halifax Building Society branch in Asda in Portie, and asked how much I needed to open an account, and was told £1-00. I handed over £1 and was asked for the account name. I said 'The Billy Graham Livelink Portobello Account'. The assistant said 'Oh, is Billy Graham coming to Portobello?' I said he would be coming by satellite broadcast if there was £600 in the account one week from today, so we were up and running. At a prayer meeting the following Wednesday, a man asked whether it was true I was hoping to put on the Livelink broadcasts, and when I said yes, he took out his cheque book, and wrote me a cheque for £400. The major problem initially was that the Portobello Town Hall was not available. A boxing promoter had booked the venue for that week. When I arrived home from the Edinburgh Council office, I had a phone call from the hall lettings lady to say that the boxing promoter had cancelled his booking in favour of Billy Graham! She must have phoned him. So it became Billy Graham Versus Beelzebub fighting contest. In the same week, someone told me to visit a housebound lady who was 'keen on Billy Graham'. She told me she and some friends were praying someone in our area would put on the meetings in our area. She went into an old handbag, and gave me some money she said her friends had sent. She used to phone me when she had a £50 pound 'lump'. She gave me a total of about £700, but she was unable to attend any of the meetings because of her arthritis.

We had more than £600 within the first week, and we signed up. I heard someone speak at a meeting I was at, and he agreed to be the chairman of the planning committee, and we formed an inter-church group to plan. We were glad when a fine Christian accountant offered to be chairman. The whole thing went like clockwork. The people who put up the satellite dish sent a man every evening in case there was a breakdown. The police were very helpful providing a 'panic button', we got a stewarding leader, and everything else we needed! The meetings lasted for a week. Two days before the end I had a phone call from a solicitor on behalf of two of his clients, offering £1500 if we were willing to say that night that our financial needs had been met. No problem! The budget was £6000. The Billy Graham outfit were extremely helpful, and never hassled us financially, or in any other way. We finished with a surplus of £3000, which we gave away to Christian causes. Several hundred people attended each evening. My main aim was that ordinary people in Portobello would have the convenient option of hearing Billy Graham preach. I am sure some people received a blessing from God.

We had five happy years serving Christ there, with one heart-breaking exception, which I'm not going to discuss. During our time in Portobello, Finlay graduated from Strathclyde University with a B.Sc. degree in Electrical and Electronic Engineering, and began work in Building Services with the Glasgow Council's Architect's Department. Janet graduated from the Queen Margaret College with a B.A. degree in Home Economics.

When Glasgow football teams visit Tynecastle or Easter Road to do battle with Hibernian or Heart of Midlothian in the beautiful game, the Edinburghers start singing about Glasgow's poor housing arrangements: 'In your Glasgow slum' and other such ditties.

(To the tune of 'In my Liverpool home')
'In your Glasgow slum, in your Glasgow slum,
You look in the dustbin for something to eat,
You find a deid cat, and you think it's a treat,
In your Glasgow slum.

In your Glasgow slum, in your Glasgow slum,
You look in Sue Ryder for something to wear,
Your wife is a junkie, your kids are in care,
In your Glasgow slum.'

Glaswegians retaliate by citing Edinburgh people's love of appearances: 'Curtains on the windows, no sheets on the beds,' and other such sayings.

It was good to live in Edinburgh, especially in the Portobello area. Edinburgh is a beautiful, mystical city, evoking a strong sense of history. There has always been a healthy rivalry between the two cities, Glasgow and Edinburgh. Edinburgh claims the history, and Glasgow claims the money, although the Edinburgh capitalists do very well by worldly standards. One of the first things the Glaswegians did when the European Commission started was put in a fund-raiser.

CHAPTER FOURTEEN –

PURE DEAD BRILLIANT

Dealing with death is one of the essentials of Christian ministry. We call it 'The King of Terrors, and the Terror of Kings', 'the Grim Reaper' and John Milton in his poem 'Lycidas' calls Death 'the blind Fury with th' abhorred shears, who slits the thin-spun life'. I was interested to read in 1 Corinthians 15 verse 26, in the apostle Paul's section on resurrection 'The last enemy to be destroyed is death'.

The Early Church Father Tertullian challenged unbelievers : 'Watch us (the Christians) how we live: watch us, how we die'. I had often thought of death as man's enemy, but the text in 1 Corinthians reveals that Death is God's enemy too. The Good News of the New Testament is that God has taken remedial action to defeat death, by sending His Son, the Lord Jesus Christ to die for our sins, and then to raise Him again to newness of life. This gives us hope beyond death .

I knew I would have to take funeral services as part of the job, so to speak. One of my earliest funerals was the funeral of a baby. He was born with two holes in the heart, and died after a few weeks of life. It was a filthy wet morning, and I will never forget the contrast between the little white coffin, and the mud-spattered surroundings of the grave. Soon after that, I had to take a funeral in a crowded home. The dead person was a young mother of five who had died of cancer, and the coffin lid was open. Throughout the service, a neighbour was stroking the dead lady's hair, and kissing her, which I thought was a bit gruesome.

Death brings you closer to families. My Principal said that we would gain more members from our funerals than anything else. He also said in relation to grief, pain and mourning that we should learn to take things to heart, rather than taking them on our hearts. I realise that we have to be professional so that we can lead a funeral service, but I see no wrong in shedding tears at a funeral service. The New Testament records three occasions when the Lord Jesus Christ wept. He wept over a city – Jerusalem, because He loves cities. He wept over a family, comforting Mary and Martha at the loss of Lazarus. Jesus loves families too. Then in the Letter to the Hebrews, it says He wept over a tyranny – the tyranny of sin and death, which He was about to deal with by going to the Cross. Regarding Jerusalem, the meaning of the Greek verb (the New Testament was written in Greek) is 'to cry loudly , or audibly'. In relation to the family, the Greek verb means 'to weep silently'. In relation to the Cross, the Hebrews letter combines strong crying (audible) and tears (silent weeping).

When an undertaker asks me to take a funeral of people I have never met, I visit their home, tell them about my life and work, then talk about the service, and finally ask questions about the dead person. I always offer to pray for them, an offer which most people accept, although I make it clear it is their choice. In one home, there was kind of stunned silence, and then the eldest son said: 'Go ahead, reverend. It'll no dae any herm, wull it?' When I finished, the matriarchal granny said: 'That wis beautiful, minister.' She then rolled up her skirt, revealing an operation scar because they had taken a vein from her leg for use in heart surgery, and said: 'Could ye pray fur ma leg, Reverend? It's giein' me gyp the day.' I said I would certainly pray for her leg, but would she mind if I didn't lay hands on it…

Funerals are opportunities to present the Good News of Jesus Christ. You are routinely faced with a gathering of people, perhaps numbering hundreds, who never normally go to church. It is of course unwise to be brutal in the presentation of the Gospel when addressing people whose hearts are sore with grief. I recently attended the funeral of a lady I knew as a lovely teenager. The minister taking the service started off with his text 'and Judas went to his place'. He immediately deduced that the place mentioned here was hell, and that most of the audience would be going there! There was no crumb of comfort for the grieving Christian parents of a young woman who had been a keen Christian in her youth. The minister also lied about his recent contacts with the lass, which were negligible in the past two or three years. I did not go to the refreshments afterwards in case I confronted the minister.

The qualitatively distinctive features of the Christian message are to me the twin facts of Christ's death, and His resurrection. The Buddhists do not claim that Siddhartha Gautama the Buddha rose from the dead, nor do the Muslims claim that Mohammed rose from the dead. The Early Church's message in the New Testament Book of Acts is: 'The God of our fathers raised Jesus from the dead –

whom you had killed by hanging Him on a tree.' (Acts 5 verse 30). I remember the Communist shop steward Jimmy Reid complaining to a Christian audience that they often spoke about the Cross without mentioning the Resurrection!

Death also brings you in contact with that unusual group of people, the undertakers. In one town where I served, there are two main undertakers. One is very tall and gaunt, with an ankle-length coat. If you were casting for the role of Count Dracula, he would be your man. He had a large pointed nose, which looks in the winter as if it were waxed. It shines like a beacon! He loved, in my early days in the town, to grasp the cuff of my suit arm, shake it a little, and whisper helpful instructions in my ear. When he acknowledged my competence at taking funerals, he grasped me one day by the cuff, and said: 'Ah'll tell ye wan thing, Doctor Mitchell – ye take a grand funeral!' What more could a body ask for? His younger name-sake functioned in the other half of town. He was a handsome fellow, who wore a top hat and sported an ebony cane with a silver top. He liked to hold ladies by both hands, gaze into their eyes and say: 'Mrs

Harestanes Baptist Church – 1993
Gary Patchen's Ordination Service

......, I have compassion for you.' The younger one used to walk out in front of the hearse into the main road , modulating his cane and controlling the traffic with great dignity and decorum. When the town built its crematorium, the younger one got the first cremation. The two undertakers were known locally as 'Coffin John' and 'Barbecue Bill'.

I realise the difficulties of taking some funerals. Since I have retired and I am without pastoral charge, most of the funerals I take are for people I do not know, and have no live church connection. I therefore go to visit these families to get to know them a little. I am able to anticipate the tension of this unknown figure – minister – coming into their home. The relief is almost palpable when you come in smiling and talk normally, asking children's names, and how long they have had their dog, and so on. I don't know what kind of ogre they were expecting; perhaps someone who will complain about them not going to church. I get the impression that they assume any minister comes from a goody-goody Christian home, and I detect a sense of relief when they learn this is not true in my case.

Let me relieve the undoubted wear and tear of discussing death by sharing some of the amusing incidents I have come across. Only the names and exact locations have been suppressed in the interests of anonymity. I must emphasise that I have entered into the sorrows as well as the more amusing aspects of some funerals.

On a musical note, one family wanted the song 'When I grow too old to dream' played for the entrance, and 'The Green Berets' Song' for exiting the church. I asked what the Green Berets' song was about, and was told it was about 'all these guys jumpin' outa aeroplanes', because the deceased liked John Wayne movies. When I expressed doubt that the organist would have the music, they said that was alright, they had a CD player. When I went with them to the local pub for refreshments, I was sitting there, all ministerial-like with the cup of tea and the wee sausage roll, a mourner came up to thank me for the 'brilliant service'. Then he said: 'Ye missed something oot, Reverend: ye never telt them he had a string vest and a bandage, and did a brilliant Rab C. Nesbitt at the New Year.' I apologised.

Another time, I was asked to ask the organist, a good singer, to sing a Scottish song as a solo at the end of the service. I said I would ask, and got a follow-up request: 'Could ye ask her to make sure she sings it before the coffin goes oot. Ah want the old guy to hear it'...

I tried to point out to one family that their choice of the second song

wasn't entirely suitable for a cremation service. 'But Mammy liked it – so we want it; she liked the 'Sing Hosanna' bit. So we sang four verses and choruses of 'give me oil in my lamp, keep me burning'.
'Tell me what your grandfather was like' I said to one lady. 'He was a rotten aul' B------' she said.
'What did he like doing?' I asked. 'Boozin' an' bettin' ' she said. At the cup of tea in the pub later, she told me she had found some of his betting slips in the drawer beside his bed, and put some into the coffin. 100 to 1 he widnae be back...
I got exactly the same 'rotten aul' B------' response in another home. The dead man's sister, when I asked her to tell me more, said he was an alcoholic. 'Tell me something else about him', I said. 'He turned ma hoose broon!' she complained. True enough – the ceilings and walls as far as I saw were coated brown with cigarette smoke. Her brother was a chain smoker who rarely went out. I finally asked her to tell me something good about her brother, and it turned out he had cared for his ill mother for the last sixteen years of her life.
'Tell me what your mother was really like', I said to one son. 'She was an unconscious comedian – she kept getting' her words mixed up. When she went into hospital with stomach problems, she told the doctor she was eatin' the same as everybody else, but it was her that caught the semolina.' (I think she got her semolina and her salmonella muxed ip).
I was dealing with two gruff and basically non-communicative Glasgow brothers. 'How did your Mother meet your father?' I asked. They briefly told me they met in Glasgow. I said, to further elicit some possibly romantic link : 'Did they meet at the dancing?' 'Naw, it widnae be the dancin' – ma da had only wan leg.' 'Oh, I'm terribly sorry' I said. The son responded with a mixture of sympathy and humour: 'That's a' right – him an' his pal used tae win the three-legged race at the school sports every year'....
I rest my case. Funerals, like the rest of life, have some shadows and some sunshine.

CHAPTER FIFTEEN –

NOW, CONCERNING THE MINISTRY

Before launching into an account of the pastorate at Kirkintilloch, I must say a few things about preaching, which to me is the core job in ministry. My involvement now stretches back over fifty-five years, since I first got on my feet to string a few sentences together as a thirteen-year old, (January 1953).

I cannot over-emphasise the role of preaching in the life of the church. I realise that it is possible to live and work as a Christian with a sense of call in any occupation. The concept of the dignity of work is a Biblical axiom from Eden onwards. Among twenty or so representative gifts listed in the New Testament, I acknowledge the importance of other functions and ministries, grace gifts and service gifts. The word-pictures of the preacher in the New Testament set preaching out in a special category. 'God was pleased through the foolishness of preaching to save those who believe' (I Corinthians 1:21). Some of the Puritans used to rank preaching with Baptism and the Lord's Supper as a third ordinance which the Lord Jesus left as an essential part of the church's continuing life. 'Jesus came… preaching' (Mark 1:14). Two of the New Testament descriptions of the preacher remind us that his authority lies outside of himself. He is a herald (verb 'kerusso', Acts 8:5) and an ambassador (verb 'presbeuo', 2 Corinthians 5:20), 'As though God were appealing to you through us.' When someone stands up to preach, his personal status is secondary and derivative. The real authority ('exousia '), what Bishop Westcott called 'rightful authority from a legitimate source' is vested in God the Father, mediated through the Lord Jesus Christ, the Son of God, and channelled to the preacher through the enabling of the Holy Spirit. Sometimes this authority is overwhelming, and mind-absorbing. One Sunday, I had prepared a sermon to preach at Findlay Memorial Tabernacle, in Maryhill Road, Glasgow, and on the way there I had a strong sense and a clear indication on my mind that I should preach instead on 'Isn't this the Carpenter?' I followed that leading, and at the end of the service, a man going out the door told me how much God had blessed him through the sermon. He told me he was a carpenter from the Western Isles, in Glasgow only for that weekend!

Phillips Brookes' definition of preaching was 'truth conveyed through personality'. The preacher is a clay vessel, merely a receptacle to hold the priceless treasure of the Gospel (2 Corinthians 4 :7), and the sum total of his life's experiences becomes the catalyst God can use to make the truth live and shine. Dr Lloyd-Jones was once asked how long it took him to prepare a particular sermon. 'Forty years' he said.

Preaching arises from personal conviction. John Bunyan, the Bedford tinker, claimed as their own by Baptists and Congregationalists alike, suffered imprisonment for about thirteen years of his life. He said, 'I preached what I did feel, what I smartingly did feel.' Real preaching is not simply a clever skill, the scientific application of homiletical principles. Obviously, there are sensible guidelines to be followed. I once received Rev G.B. Duncan's permission to sit in on a lecture he gave to students in the Bible Training Institute, on his preaching method. His simple analysis has fuelled many a session of preparation for me, and I suppose for others. Since he has gone home to be with the Lord, I pass it on:

1. Analyse the Text. Use lexicons, Bible dictionaries, commentaries

Portobello Festival Victorian Weekend – Portobello High Street

and translations to establish its meaning.

2. Organise the Truth. Arrange the material in clearly-defined, logical, and digestible packages. To use an analogy, 'deliver your coal in sacks' rather than 'dumping a ton on people's doorsteps'.

3. Humanise the Telling. Illustrate the message with human examples. Give the truth 'legs', so that you make living the Christian life a viable option in today's world. Illustrations in a talk are like windows in a building, giving it light and air.

Preaching has the highest aims. The preacher's task has been defined as ' Waking the dead in half an hour', although he can never be more than the Holy Spirit's vehicle in this.

The Victorian era was the golden age of the pulpiteers, who thundered out the truth, but often lived bizarre lives outside the pulpit and were sometimes sad, isolated figures. In the Greek text of Ephesians 4:11, one definite article covers both descriptions, 'pastors and teachers' indicating a partnership role in these functions in the Body of Christ which is the Church. Ray Stedman compares the role of pastor/teacher in the Church to the cleansing function of the liver and kidneys in our physical bodies. They are there to flush out the system, to assist in the removal of undesirable impurities.

It means that the mutual functions of pastor and teacher enhance the ministry of each. When you can look out on a congregation on a Sunday, no matter how busy a week it has been, and know that you have been pastorally involved with some of them that week, it 'earths' the Biblical truth you are trying to teach. Becoming involved in the lives of others is precious but energy-sapping, a delicate but potentially dangerous work. The dangers are that people depend on you for verdicts and decisions when your knowledge of circumstances is very patchy and incomplete, and that you are exposing yourself to misunderstanding. To love is to be vulnerable. Ministers are imperfect people in a perfection-ridden context. Being a pastor guards against your preaching and teaching becoming a sterile, theoretical exercise, where you can be playing theological games, answering questions that the people are not asking. Too many preachers went from school to University, and then to denominational college. They were launched into becoming a church minister with virtually no experience of everyday life and work. This has several unhelpful consequences. First of all, they have difficulty relating to ordinary working folk in their struggles and trials. Secondly, some of them produce sermons that are like buildings without windows, preaching without illustrating how

Biblical truth can be related to everyday life.

Thirdly, they become sympathetic to 'ministerial/lay' division which isolates them from their people.

Fourthly, they can subscribe to the 'specialist' rather than the 'general practitioner' view of ministry. Some become big enough in the head to think they can live above contradiction, criticism, or correction. They may even go over to a 'chief executive officer' view of ministry, which will excuse them from visiting their people, and to excuse them from the steady routine of preaching the Word of God.

As I write, I visualise a small white coffin being gently lowered into a mud-spattered grave in Fife in winter, or a half-night spent in Yorkhill Hospital, Glasgow, praying to God with a young couple that their baby's life should be spared (it was), or sitting in a home in the aftermath of a funeral, trying to comfort a widow left alone after more than fifty years with a husband she loved deeply.

I find preaching stimulating and fascinating, but sometimes tiring.. Although I was eighteen years out of what is formally known as 'the ministry', I preached regularly throughout these eighteen years, mainly in churches of the Baptist persuasion.

What is a Baptist church? It is a local expression of the body of Christ, a gathered fellowship of believers, constituted and guided

Lunch 'n' Listen, Inverness, August 2000
Jean, George, Nancy, Jessie and Sheila

141

by the Holy Spirit. Its early pastors were unpaid, and some of the earliest churches (in England) were Particular Baptist churches, i.e. they believed in Christ's particular redemption, so that the atonement was limited in its application to the elect. Some of the earlier churches were, by contrast, 'General Baptist Churches'. Some churches had a 'closed-membership, closed-table' policy on communion. The majority of Scottish Baptist churches now have a 'closed-membership, open-table' policy. Baptist churches are not ruled by external or internal hierarchies. About ninety of the one-hundred and ten New Testament references to the church refer to local churches. The decision-making body is the church meeting, with the gathered fellowship seeking the mind of Christ in its decision-making. The Baptist Diaconate (group of elected deacons) is an executive body. The term 'Deacons' Court' is a misleading misnomer, since a court generally produces decisions which are binding on others. In most churches, the present practice is to have a periodic election of deacons. A few churches appoint elders as well as deacons, but in most fellowships, some leaders have eldership functions. The Baptist Union of Scotland is a fellowship of churches, not a governing body, and Baptist ministers are, in general, paid by their own congregation, not from a central fund.

The Baptist churches I have served in are: Fulham (London, Sunday

Portobello Baptist Church – 1984-89

School teacher), Edmonton (London, student pastor), Buckhaven (Fife, pastor), Springburn (Glasgow, deacon), Kirkintilloch Townhead (deacon), Portobello (Edinburgh, pastor), Kirkintilloch Harestanes (pastor), and Inverness (Castle Street, pastor). I have preached in about seventy of the Baptist churches in Scotland.

When I was working at Smithycroft School, I had served as Kirkintilloch Baptist Church's deacon for the Harestanes district. We started a Sunday School there in the community centre, had a summer mission there for the children of the district, and eventually (after I left for Portobello) there was a fine (Roman Catholic) janitor appointed who was willing to be on duty if we rented the school for Sunday services. There was intensive visitation of the district, and the work grew. Imagine my delight to have an invitation to preach for the initial pastorate at Harestanes! It was like going home. Harestanes was a Glasgow overspill estate in Kirkintilloch, with carefully selected tenants from Glasgow Council housing lists. The houses were built by the Scottish Special Housing Association (later known as Scottish Homes). The adjacent Langmuir estate, which consisted of Wimpey owner-occupied houses, took the population to about 7,000. There were no other churches nearby. I was like a kid in a candy store when we were called there in September 1989.

The Community Centre next to the Primary School had been surplus classroom units, and was able to be rented from the Community Centre committee, most of whom were Baptist church members. The church membership was forty when we went, and ninety-two when we left, after six years there. We had a Boys' Brigade Company with ninety boys, and built up a Girls' Campaigner group to around fifty girls attending each week. I had three Primary school chaplaincies in Kirkintilloch, at Gartconner, Hillhead, and Harestanes.

During our time at Harestanes, I completed studies for the Ph.D. degree with Trinity Theological Seminary, Indiana, which is now linked in Britain for external studies with Liverpool University. It was back to the '5 am-till-midnight' stint, for about three and a half years. For purposes of comparison, some of their courses, particularly in Old Testament Archaeology, History of Philosophy, and Philosophy of Religion, were of the highest calibre, at least as good as anything we have in Britain.

During our time at Harestanes, we faced some major financial difficulties as a family. We thought we had done our homework, had sought good advice, and prayed hard, before venturing into business.

Jean and Janet went into partnership in a catering venture, but we had to close down the coffee shop/sweet shop which Jean and Janet had run for four years the work was killing them. We lost all our savings and found ourselves (no one else) in considerable debt. We concluded that clearly it was our responsibility - we should not look for 'handouts'. It was a case of going back to the Lord who had financed me through London Bible College, and everything else since, and humbly asking for His help. In answer to prayer, I was given the means through which God provided the funds since then to help us out of our mess. I was offered lecturing for one Saturday morning per month, invited to preach at a Convention, given the opportunity to be an examiner for GCSE, and in other amazing ways, by the time we left Harestanes in 1995, we were debt-free, and saving like mad for a retirement property. The situation in Baptist ministry at that time was that there was no guarantee of help towards retirement housing. Ministers sometimes put their name on a council waiting list, and hoped for the best. Due to Mrs Thatcher's encouragement to council house tenants to buy the house they were in, many people took advantage of this, so the stock of available council housing reduced dramatically. There was a Baptist Ministers' Retirement Property Fund, which bought up property with money left in legacies, or gifted by generous families, and as funds were available ministers could pay a deposit, and a reasonable rent to the Fund, and enjoy security of tenure during the lifetimes of the minister and his wife. After their deaths, the property reverted to the Fund, and the family were repaid the original deposit (no interest added). I realised this would be a difficulty, since about ten ministers would be retiring in the same year as me.

A far more serious blow hit us when Janet took ill while serving as a nanny in America. She was flown home, and eventually had excellent care through her major surgery in the Southern General Hospital in Glasgow. She made a full recovery. I had the privilege of conducting the marriage services of both of our children while we were at Harestanes.

I had an invitation to be nominated for the Vice-Presidency of the Baptist Union in 1993, and declined. There was a good man already 'in the field', and I had no intention of running against him.

In 1994 I was approached again, and this time I let my nomination go forward, so that I was to become President at the Inverness Assembly, held at Eden Court Theatre in October 1995.

In 1995 I had an invitation to consider preaching for the vacancy at the Baptist Church in Castle Street, Inverness. After an initial refusal for what I thought were two sound reasons, another letter came from Inverness. After prayer and sharing with the Harestanes elders, I went to preach, and received a strong call from the congregation. So we went to live in the beautiful city of Inverness. It achieved city status while we were there. The first year I was there as minister, I was away a lot on Presidential duties (covering about 20,000 miles in the car).

My comments on ministry must be rounded off with an expression of gratitude to God for His grace and goodness. He has never failed me, although at times I have occasionally been dreadfully disappointed in His earthly representatives. He has been so kind to me in giving me a stable childhood, rich in opportunities to play, read, learn, and enter into life. It is also a relief to know, these days, that I was never abused as a child. The Lord has given me a genuine experience of Himself, which has helped my learning curve with myself, and with other people. God has also given me a terrific family life. We are grateful to God for our children, our daughter-in- law Fiona, and son-in-law Billy, and for our grandchildren Kirstin and Angus. Kirstin is now ten years old, and Angus is six.

If you have read my story so far, I hope you concede that my outlook is generally realistic, positive and hopeful. I am sorry that I cannot be entirely positive in my comments about the church and the ministry. I would emphasise that negative experiences are very small in number, like a few 'dead flies which give perfume a bad smell' (Ecclesiastes 10: I). I have sometimes wondered whether my non-Christian background has meant that my expectations of Christians have been too high, which has led to great personal disappointment in people. I don't think so, because my wide knowledge of human nature has made me aware of the decency of the ungodly, which is of course part of God's providence. I emerge from my experience in the formal ministry bruised, but unbowed in my conviction that it is not unreasonable to expect loyalty and integrity from fellow-believers and fellow-workers in God's church. I have occasionally tried to salvage colleagues from total despair at the treatment they have received as pastors from church members and leaders. We are all sinners. It is perhaps a sign of the Holy Spirit's presence in a church that it attracts the unlovely, the neurotic fringe, and the power-brokers and control freaks no-one else can suffer. This, of course, makes life more difficult for ministers. No wonder the fall-out rate is so high! One of the great sadnesses is that the fine, quiet Christian people who form the majority in Baptist churches allow situations to develop so that they become led by the power-brokers and control freaks. They should speak out at their church meetings, for they have nothing to lose but their chains. Unfortunately, in my view, church meetings, Baptist Union Councils, and Baptist Assemblies have become 'rubber stamp' kind of meetings devoid of the cut-and-thrust of debate and discussion we used to know.

A friend of mine in school-teaching was principal teacher of guidance. He told me that at regular intervals, he had what he called a 'Jimmy McGregor Week'. 'Who's Jimmy McGregor?' you may ask. 'That's the whole point, , John would reply. 'Jimmy McGregor is the boy who gets washed and dressed to come to school. He does his homework, behaves well with fellow-pupils and teachers, and actually enjoys school.' Ten per cent of the school take up eighty per cent of the time of teachers doing guidance. Jimmy McGregor is one of the ninety per cent. I think we should have 'Jimmy McGregor' weeks in the ministry, devoted to the members of the congregation who love the church and respect the minister, and are happy to be involved in the church's life in the community.

The 'command structure' in Baptist ministry is not clear, and in the absence of a bishop or a presbytery for back-up, a lot devolves on the minister. Personal issues sometimes escalate into power struggles. The willingness of believers in the past to acquiesce with majority decisions has given way to individuals asserting themselves at church meetings. The 'cafeteria' outlook has become insidious, so that people who do not find what they want 'on the menu', so to speak, will not only go elsewhere, but will make an awful fuss before they leave.

Another feature of being a preacher is that it disrupts weekends! I like to have Saturday evenings free of meetings, so that I can be like a boxer at training camp, getting ready for the big fight with Beelzebub on Sundays. On the credit side, there is no feeling so delicious as on a Sunday after the evening service when you feel you have given your best, and God has blessed both preacher and hearers in the living experience of the presence of God, and the reality of his Word. I have often said that the ministry must be one of the few occupations where you are loved by the people you work for. It is an incomparable joy to work with a congregation as God's servant.

My story started at Rottenrow, Glasgow. My final experience as a Baptist minister was about 170 miles away, in Inverness. The Inverness Rottenrow was any row in the stand, watching Inverness Caley Thistle, and they're not a bad team. My first experience of Inverness football was being invited to join one of our members to a Saturday game, before the club moved to the present stadium. My friend insisted that he was paying me in. When we got to the turnstile, he asked for tickets for two senior citizens! I was a mere 56 years old at this point, so I put on a stoop and affected a limp, not wishing to embarrass my friend. The worst aspect, I thought, was that no-one challenged me. But there was worse to come, because he asked me at half-time could I give him the programme I had bought, as there was a lucky programme draw! By Sunday lunch-time, the tables of the Baptists were rocking with the story of how I had got into the game as a senior citizen. The club moved into their own stadium, and won promotion to the First Division. It was quiet enough to be sitting in church, and the football was not of the same standard that I was used to. I kept wanting to jump the barrier and offer help, or go like a Trekkie after the game and claim my money under the Trades Description Act: 'this is not football as we know it.' Absence made the heart grow fonder, especially on Saturday afternoons.

Where were we going to retire to? Ministers are rootless beings on retirement. Those who stay on in the area where they last ministered can create problems for the church and for their successor. Someone told me that there were some vacant houses in Drumchapel, Glasgow.

Mmmmm. ...

CHAPTER SIXTEEN –

THINKING BLACK

My earliest experiences as a Christian at Lambhill Mission made me aware of what was called 'The Mission Field'. Missionaries were held in the highest esteem, and were sometimes spoken of in hushed tones. The Mission had a monthly missionary meeting. We sang missionary hymns which many folk today would reckon smacked of Imperialist Victorian Britain:

'Far far away in heathen darkness dwelling,
Millions of souls for ever may be lost;
Who, who will go, salvation's story telling,
Looking to Jesus, counting not the cost'

Annie Thomson was one of several members who went overseas as missionaries. Annie worked in Congo.

We also had Miss Spearman from a missionary society in India, and Henry T Reid, who was nicknamed 'high tension' Reid because of his energetic presentation of Christian work among the Jews.

Bill Johnstone, a Springburn man, worked with his wife Cathie in Brazil among primitive tribes-people. He was sent up the Amazon to investigate the disappearance of the 'three Freds' who were Christian martyrs in the Amazon jungle. Mr Johnstone used to bring along South American Indian bows and arrows. He once brought home a monkey, which created such havoc in their home that they gave it to Wilson's Zoo in Oswald Street, near the Central Station.

We had a visit once from an outstanding Ulster missionary called Fred Orr, who was only with us one Sunday, but made a tremendous impact, especially on the young people. He worked initially with the Worldwide Evangelization Crusade and later worked with the Acre Gospel mission. He was travelling up the Amazon by dugout canoe on the final stage of his journey to his first assignment, when his wife died, and his first duty there was to bury his wife.

Lambhill Mission did not have a pastor, so we had preaching visits from the Scottish deputation secretaries of Missionary societies. They generally gave some information of the areas their society worked in, some of them spoke well from Scripture, and some of them had served overseas as missionaries. Jock Purves, who became Vice-President of the Worldwide Evangelization Crusade, used to come to preach at both services on two Sundays in the year. He was a godly, canny Scot who had seen missionary service in the remote parts of north India, near the Khyber Pass. He wrote two good books about the Scottish Covenanters ('Fair Sunshine' and Sweet Believing'). He wrote about the Shotts Kirk Revival of 1630, and a book called 'The Unlisted Legion', about Christian work in Karakoram and the Khyber. He was a fascinating man, with an amazing breadth of knowledge.

Gilbert Campbell was the Scottish secretary for the Regions Beyond Missionary Union, which worked in Peru, Congo, India, and Irian Jaya (formerly Dutch New Guinea, Indonesia). Gilbert and his wife Ella, members of the Findlay Memorial Church near St George's Cross, had served for about twenty-five years in Congo. Gilbert was in the building trade, especially good at bricklaying. I am sure some of the churches he built will still be standing. When he came home on furlough once he brought a Congolese knife to be used as a bread knife by his parents, who lived in Buccleuch Street, above Charing Cross. One Saturday night, Gilbert wrapped the knife in newspaper, and set off to walk from Kirklee Crescent off Great Western Road, to take it to his Mum and Dad. At that time there was a dance hall in St George's Road called the West End Ballroom, set above the main road up a long stairway. Sadly, this place had a reputation for mayhem and brawling, especially on Saturday evenings, with the warring factions often spilling down the stairs on to the pavement, and even the main road. Well, the godly Gilbert was carefully skirting the crowd, when a police wagon arrived, and Gilbert was 'lifted' as the Glaswegians say, and ushered into the police office. When they unwrapped his parcel, Gilbert was asked for an explanation for having this ugly African killing weapon. He said: 'Well, actually, I'm a missionary home from the Congo, and this has to be my father's bread-knife.' The policeman told him to 'shut up and get into that cell'. Gilbert had to send for his father to bail him out, and the police were churlish enough to keep the 'bread-knife'.

I had a lot of dealings with Gilbert because I attended a monthly prayer meeting in his home, served with him on the Scottish Council of the RBMU for fifteen years, and I helped to organise the Missionary Youth Conference. Gilbert told me once he believed that God had made the personalities of the people He called to suit the cultures where God sent them to serve. He told me I was definitely suited to Africa...When I went to be pastor of Inverness Baptist Church, two of my former students, Ronnie and Margaret Sim, were teaching in Nairobi, Kenya. They had served in Ethiopia for years, and were now teaching at the Nairobi Evangelical School of Theology. Doctor Ronnie was a linguistic specialist, teaching the skills of Bible translation, and Margaret was teaching Greek. They were staff members of the Summer Institute of Linguistics, or Wycliffe Bible Translators. Ronnie had to go out for some committee meetings, and he suggested that I should come with him. I had met another former student of mine at the Keswick Convention, and he told me about a College he had visited, Scott Theological College, in Machakos, Kenya, formerly an Africa Inland Mission College (now Scott Christian University) but now with University status, chartered by the Kenya government. He said that I would love it, and that I should contact the Principal if ever I was visiting Kenya. Ronnie was involved in committees for three days, and I e-mailed the Principal, and arranged to teach some lessons in Greek grammar, and a few lectures on the Greek text of 1 John in the New Testament. I had a great time, and was invited back for eight years to be a member of a lecturing team of four, doing a Block Unit (40 lecture periods in ten days). There was a retired Philosophy professor, a Psychology Ph.D, a Biblical Theology person, and yours truly doing the Gospels most years. Each of us would teach a different year group, and see the same class each day. We would assess, grade and win the students a few semester hours towards their BA degree, then crawl on to the nearest plane home.

It was worth the four-and-a-half thousand mile journey. Kenya is a beautiful country. No matter what the journey was like, there would be Douglas the College driver, smiling at the exit from Jomo Kenyatta Airport, ready to take me on the two-hour drive down the Mombasa road, and off into the wilds until we reached the large town of Machakos, 64 kilometres south-east of Nairobi. The Mombasa road has a spiritual but scary influence on travellers. It makes heaven seem nearer! There are potholes galore, and no hard shoulder, so that lorries in a hurry can leave the edge of the crumbling tarmac, overtake on the dirt on the left, covering your windscreen with dust, and then veering right in front of you... They say the road is improving, but since they reckon about a third of the

Kenya budget goes on graft, corruption and bribery, there isn't much money left for public works. The lorries and the matatus (minibuses) often bear English Premiership team slogans, or Biblical texts, or both. There is supposed to be a maximum number limit on the minibus, but I counted 19 people in mine one day. I watched the efforts to shove what we called in Glasgow 'a sturdy burdie' into our minibus, and then read the text: 'With God all things are possible'. Machakos was the first administrative centre for the British colony, built in 1887, about ten years before Nairobi. The centre moved to Nairobi largely because the railway from Mombasa was completed, mainly by Indian workers, and Nairobi was more central. Machakos is a busy place, and is a strong banking centre. Scott Theological College was named after the founder of the African Inland Mission, a Scot called Peter Cameron Scott, who died about a year later. The College is about two miles from Machakos, at the foot of a lovely hill. The British ruled Kenya with efficiency and some cruelty, without going into too much unsavoury detail. After the Mau Mau uprising in the fifties, the country was granted Independence, and Jomo Kenyatta the Kikuyu chief was turned from a 'poacher' into a 'game-keeper' as President after Independence in 1963. Kenya gained some stability, and a reputation as the African success story, with glorious beaches on the Indian Ocean, happy smiling Africans to say 'Jambo' and 'Karibu' to, and excellent safari and film-making prospects, like 'Elsa the Lioness', Out of Africa', and 'White Mischief'. The great spin-off from a Christian missions point of view was that public education is still conducted in English. Apart from a false assumption that I was American, the Africans had no problem understanding educated Scots. On one of my earlier visits, a young American said :

'Say, brother Mitchell, will we have to provide an interpreter for your strange Scots dialect?' I replied: 'Listen, sonny: Scottish missionaries were educating Africans when you lot were busily skinning Red Indians!'

Every Kenyan student in my classroom spoke at least three languages – Kiswahili the trade language, English the language of education, and the local language of his town or village.

My first impressions were varied and interesting. On the first day, when the College Principal drove us in to have lunch in a Machakos restaurant, as the car drew into the car park, we were aware of children round the car, begging. In the early days, I was around the

College office to have lecture notes run off, and was slightly annoyed that the girls in the office wouldn't look at me when I was talking to them. I soon learned that this was a hangover from the colonial days: it was bold and rude for an African girl to speak to you eye to eye or face to face. On another occasion, I gave money to a young woman to help with her rent, and she grasped her dress and curtsied to me! I like to visit local churches – there are about four thousand African Inland Churches, each with its diocese and bishop, and another early impression was the sheer size and obvious numerical growth of the churches. In Scotland, we are in what the Bible calls 'the day of small things', with a general decline in church membership and church attendance. In January 2011, I took the first of a series of preachers' workshops for the African pastors, at the Jericho AIC. They invited me to preach on the Sunday morning at the English service from 9-11 am and at the Kiswahili service through an interpreter from 11am -1pm. They told me later that they had about one thousand six hundred at the English service, and about seventeen hundred at the Kiswahili service – 3300 in one morning!

I have not been mugged or threatened or robbed during my visits, but another early impression was a sense of danger. I was living for a few days at the Africa Inland Mission Guest House in Nairobi, Mayfield Lodge. The lady missionary who drove me about advised me not to go out, or if I did, not to take any rings, watches or jewellery, no credit cards, or cash other than what I needed. She said she sometimes saw men going home in their underwear. I had visions of the effect on the old lady missionaries at the Guest House were I to appear at the front door in my Y-fronts... City streets have bandidos in plenty, and they don't all wear masks. I was told that some of them were ruled by politicians. Every building of repute has walls or security fences, locking gates, and guards 24/7.

Some banks have armed guards outside, and riot sticks placed on the counters inside. Nairobi is nicknamed 'Nairobbery'. Car-jackings and housebreak-ins often end in murder, so that victims cannot become witnesses.

Generally, there are three ways out of the pit of poverty for an African young person. The first is to become a pop star. The second is to become a football star. The third is to become an academic star, and heap up the pieces of paper in the form of academic qualifications. In the classroom, I was made immediately aware of this. The first questions they wanted answers for were where you trained, what level of qualifications you had, who were your teachers, and what contacts you had with great preachers teachers, or good colleges or universities. The Kenyans are desperate for academic success, for themselves and their children. Children of College staff would leave for school about 6.30am. When they got to school, they had to sit for an hour until the teacher came, although teachers were on a rota to monitor the building. If children arrived in anything but 100% school uniform, they were sent home. I have seen mothers weeping because they didn't have enough money to buy school uniform. School fees figure largely in family budgets, and then there is the cost of transport, meals and text-books. Students and staff at the College were always trying to find sponsors for their children's education.

I met a few students in my classes who would match anyone in Britain, although the average standard of written English was probably lower than you would want. The College library was open until ten o'clock at night. There would be about eighty students working in the library at 9.30pm any evening. (there were about 130 students).

Another impression was the growing awareness of poverty. There was a Kamba village about half a mile from Scott College gate. I watched the people walking the two miles each way to and from Machakos, and my straw poll revealed that about a third of them were barefoot, about a third had flip-flops, and the remainder had a wide range of footwear. At the morning break I bought a poor odd-job man a drink and a bun from the College kiosk, and when I asked him on the third morning what he would like, he said 'bread, please'. I got him three slices of dry bread and what Glaswegians call an 'ootsider', the end slice of a loaf, and he scoffed it in about two minutes flat. One day around five o'clock, I was at the gate, and asked someone to buy a bunch of bananas from the Kamba village fruit barrow at the gate. There were six or seven bananas in the bunch (20 pence in British money), and when I shared them out, they disappeared very quickly, as if the guys around the gate were hungry. I have visited families where there was literally nothing to eat in the house. The local livestock were showing their ribs, and the student food did not look very nutritious. They liked stuff called ugali, which looked and tasted like a cross between polystyrene and solidified wallpaper paste. It was probably some sort of root with the goodness beaten out of it, but it felt filling as it lay in the stomach like cement.

In Nairobi, you have the greatest possible contrast between the rich context of the lovely Java House, or Karen Country Club, and the cut-throat rat-race in unspeakable slums like Kibera, with its streams of raw sewage, and its clouds of wood-fire smoke where you could almost cut a slice of the fetid smell of excrement hanging in the air.

There were one or two exception to this 'hamely fare'. There was an occasional goat feast. A wee goat would be playing around the College grounds, unaware that at noon it would be trussed up, killed, stripped of its innards, and by three o'clock it had been cooked, and was being served up, with brains on a plate as a special treat for the children!

Secondly, one Sunday, I was invited to preach at the home church of a College security man, and afterwards to go to his home for lunch. He had been telling me that in the few weeks before my visit, his cow had a calf, and his nanny goat had a kid, so he was now the proud owner of three cows, three goats, and six hens. After lunch we were walking around, and I said: 'Robert, I can see your three goats and your three cows, but I can only see five chickens'. 'We've just eaten the other one' he said. I suppose the cockerel would be proud to have a son 'in the ministry' so to speak…

There were a lot of amusing interludes. I was taken golfing to the Machakos golf club, where they have browns instead of greens, and the fairways were needing a bit of attention. We paid for two Kenyan lads to caddy for us. I thought of them as 'golden retrievers', but even they could not find one particular ball. As we all searched in the rough for the ball, the cry went up: 'Pincer ants'. We all rushed up to the next tee, where I was told to drop my trousers and kill all ants advancing up my legs. Apparently, they seem to cause great pain and havoc if they reach the genital areas. At the end of it all, as we stood there in our underpants, I shared my thought with my partners, that we must surely have contravened the dress code for the course.

At the end of each visit, I began to feel like Jesus, for they seemed to be casting lots over my garments! Jean had hardly any washing to do on my return, although I never got any requests for my underwear. I would go home with much less than I took, and they would discuss who was getting shirts, pullovers or shoes. One of the guards got a pair of Dunlop tennis shoes, only twenty-three years old, and with no holes in the soles. When I came back the following year, there he was, wearing my shoes, whitened up, and with new laces. About half-way through my stay he said: 'I saw you were wearing white shoes the first two days'…pregnant pause…. 'my feet haven't grown since last year'...pregnant pause... 'I was hoping to up-grade my shoes this year'. I said: 'I'm sorry, it's so-and-so's turn this year'... pregnant pause...'But you gave them to me last year'...

The roots of discontent go down deep, back to the time Kenya was, like Algeria, South Africa and Southern Rhodesia, almost White Man's Country. White farmers in Kenya grew rich during World War II, and the Mau Mau trouble started after the War. By the time the struggle ended, and Jomo Kenyatta emerged from jail and became President, about 16,800 people were killed. During the rebellion Britain hanged more than 1000 Kenyans by 1963..

Kenya almost had its only successful coup in 1982, when Daniel Arap

Robert, The Watchman – Machakos, Kenya – 2005

Moi was President. There was also a string of unsolved murders of dissident politicians since 1983 – JM Kariuki, Tom Mboya, and Robert Ouko. About 150 were killed in the events of 1982.

In 2008, Kenya erupted, at the time of elections, and about a thousand people were killed. My family did not want me to go, but the main trouble was in Nairobi, and Eldoret. In the Machakos area, a local politician came promising bread, speaking to a crowd of several hundred near the College gate. There was a local issue about re-routing a road, and putting up a fence, but he came threatening trouble. When I came out of class I heard gunfire. The politician had a big car with loud-speaking equipment, and was rousing the crowd, but there was a police presence. The Scott students went to the chapel and prayed. The crowd passed the college, and were later dispersed in Machakos town centre, using tear gas.

AIDS (Acquired Immune Deficiency Syndrome) is a terrible problem in Africa. One in five families in Nairobi is being brought up by a child because the parents have died of AIDS. Despite what many people have been told, many people dying of AIDS have been celibate before marriage, and faithful since – infected by partners, or medical treatment with infected blood or dirty needles. Dr Patrick Dixon writes: 'If you know ten people in your town or city have died of AIDS , it means between 250 and 1000 are walking around the streets every day feeling fine, but carrying the killer virus.' AIDS spreads like wildfire, although the spread through sexual contact is slow compared to the spread from injecting drugs, because most people do not swop partners every day of every week. By the end of 2007, about 22.5 million Africans living south of the Sahara Desert were living with AIDS. In East and Central Africa, the prevalence is 10-20%. South Africa has about one-sixth of the global total of victims. Average life expectancy in Southern and East Africa in 1950 was about forty years. In 1990 it was about fifty-five. It is now below forty again. When a family breadwinner dies, it is a double whammy for the family – loss of income and funeral debts. Widows find that the dead husband's family can grab her inheritance, and she and her children become destitute. On her death, her daughters become school dropouts, and the impoverished victims of men who make them pregnant with HIV-positive babies, and the whole of the local area is caught up in what Richard Dowden calls 'a downward spiral of death and deprivation'. Men in the armed forces often have many sexual partners either at gunpoint or in return for favours. Some reports suggested that the rate of HIV (Human Immunodeficiency Virus, a retro-virus which causes AIDS) infection in some sections of the Kenya army is up to 90%. We in Britain are not without sin. The spread of sexually transmitted diseases is exponential. Gonorrhoea continues to spread and is increasingly resistant to drugs. There is no cure for herpes, a recurrent problem whose symptoms include painful blisters, making sex impossible. Cervical (neck of the womb) cancer is more common because more girls have their first sex as teenagers, and have a number of different partners. Binge drinking fuels the fire. More and more women find they cannot have children because their insides have been damaged by sexual disease. The so-called wonderful sex age we live in has left Britain with millions of casualties.

In Africa, things are exacerbated by two curses. Firstly, in the rural areas, there is quite often an experienced man in the village who is used to initiate girls in sexual matters, and infects them. Secondly, although the practice of female circumcision, which amounts to female mutilation, is banned by law, it continues secretly to compound

Jersey – 1997

Machakos, Kenya – 2011

the misery suffered by girls and women. I know of a girl in her late teens, who escaped from her village to avoid this disgusting rite, and was lured back by her family, and forced to be circumcised. She wept for months.

Christians are now leading the fight against AIDS in many nations. Archbishop Desmond Tutu estimated churches and Christian organisations are providing over 60% of HIV community programmes in Africa. This shocks some people who cannot understand how Christians can be involved in committed caring while unable to endorse certain lifestyles. Dr Patrick Dixon, a world expert on HIV/AIDS writes: 'those with AIDS are lepers of today facing fear and rejection. When Jesus touched a leper, He made history – still talked about over 2000 years later….Many people with AIDS today are dying without hope and without God. I think of our Heavenly Father, tears pouring down His face, not wanting any to perish, nor to be separated one day more, yet with sadness releasing people to go their own way.'

I am sorry to lift the lid on the sad side of African life, but there are many happy sides. The Kenyans are not only great runners, they are great, resilient people, amazingly optimistic. They have a wonderful country. Kenya has been a black hole for Western money, which in some quarters has bred a dependency culture, but there is some terrific work going on , which encourages them to make use of their own resources and climate. They have great potential income from rose-growing, fish-farming and mushroom farming, from improved methods of animal husbandry, and so on. The growth and image of Christianity in the Kenyan communities is much more positive than in Britain, and the people are great fun to be with. Gilbert Campbell was right – I was meant for Africa, even although I have made just a few short visits. My visual style of preaching and teaching suited them. Humour as always is a good servant and a bad master. My students once asked me why John Stott was a bachelor. The Kenyans seemed to think you were not fully a man unless you were married. I listed a few possible explanations – perhaps the desirable was unobtainable, and the obtainable was undesirable, or perhaps the girl he liked had a formidable mother who frightened him off. I said: 'In Scotland, we say, that if you are thinking on marrying the kitten, have a look at the cat!' That brought the house down... On Hogmanay, 31 December 2008, I conducted the funeral of a wee boy who lived in the West of Glasgow. Billy was eleven years old, with spina bifida,and other problems. I was leaving for Kenya on New Years Day. In the summer of 2007, Billy wanted to go to Benidorm, his favourite holiday resort, because above all he wanted to swim with the dolphins. His dad, a taxi driver, couldn't get insurance for Billy – so he drove him to Benidorm, and he swam with the dolphins! On Hogmanay night 2008, I had a phone call from Billy's dad, thanking me for various things. Then he said he knew I could help him. Three weeks before wee Billy died, he and his dad had been watching a TV documentary about an African orphanage. When the programme finished, Billy said he felt sorry for the African children, and could his dad take all the money out of his bank and send it to Africa? His dad said to me that the family, (post-funeral and on Hogmanay) were in no fit state to bring me the money. Could I come and collect it? I went over and when Jean and I counted the money at home, there was a sum of £600 in the envelope. I knew about Springs of Hope Children's Care, about a mile from the College gate, and the Enendeni Project, an orphanage in the Kamba village about half a mile from the College gate in the other direction. I divided the £600

Family Grouop 2010 – Billy, George and Finlay,
Janet, Angus, Jean, Kirstin and Fiona

equally, and gave it to the two groups. Mary, a trained nurse ran Springs of Hope, with about fifty children there, and the Enendeni Project looked after village children whose parents had died of AIDS. It was run by a committee whose chair person was Joyce, a lady on the College staff. When I returned to Scotland, I told the story of Billy in a children's talk, about the lad in John chapter 6 who gave his five loaves and two small fish to Jesus, and blessed about five thousand people. A married couple in the congregation have been sending money for the orphans ever since. I have received cheques for several hundred pounds, and sent the money out from the local travel agent in Kirkintilloch.

I visited Springs of Hope Children's Care in January 2011, and spoke with Mary. She rents the place they are in, but she has bought the piece of land next to it. She put up a perimeter fence, and had a bore-hole dug for water supply. When she told me her next move was to put up a building, I asked how much money she would need. She thought about a million Kenya shillings. I said we would pray about that.

A week after I came home, I was speaking at a ladies' meeting. After the meeting, a lady came out to the car park, and said she wanted to buy two of my books, but they were sold out. I said that if she gave me her address, I would send the books to her the following day. I posted the books, and the following week, the lady sent a short note, with a cheque for £5000! (I should say, I wasn't speaking about Kenya at the meeting, but the chair person had told the ladies I was just back from Kenya where I had been doing workshops, giving seminars, and visiting orphans). About ten days later, the donor came to see us, and brought another cheque, for £1000! I had her permission for the money to be used to build an orphanage. Two weeks later, another lady wrote to me. She and her husband had missed my visit to their church, but they had been encouraged by the CD of the service, and she enclosed a cheque for £1000! To summarise, since the end of January until the end of March, I have sent about 900,000 Kenya shillings. It is in the Springs of Hope bank account, and they can start building. Mary sent me a verbal description of her 'dream' about the new premises, and some architectural drawings. God is still alive, and is interested and involved in Africa!

My visits to Kenya started in 2001, and have continued until 2011. As I close this piece of writing, I am almost 72 years old. I recently went to see a film 'The King's Speech', and found Colin Firth's portrayal of King George VI's speech difficulties very moving, as I have spent a lot of my life 'earning my living by hollering' as a pearly king from London put it. I went out of the cinema grateful to God that I am still able to speak and preach and teach. The diary is still busy. Jean now makes me write in telephone numbers for the engagements I take on, so that will ease her burden if I take ill or die! It's not that she has become suddenly pessimistic. She was always a realist. When I started jogging in the 1980s she made me take out a ten-pence coin to phone for help if I ran out of puff, and my home phone number in case I collapsed. At the moment, I aim to continue, and I wouldn't mind being like Errol Flynn, and those who 'died with their boots on'.

POSTSCRIPT 1

Christian Focus have kindly asked me to write an up-date on the book. The expectation was that 'Comfy Glasgow' would have a shelf-life of around a year, and sell a few thousand copies, and here we are on the third reprint - three-and-a-half-years later.

The book has certainly travelled. I have had letters from missionaries in Africa, an American girl in Hong Kong, a pastor in Australia, a fellow-pupil from South Africa, and so on. There have been long letters from people in Scotland, noting points of contact. I have had long telephone calls from old friends, and I have established contact with my old Primary school teacher's widow. A family from Culloden, Inverness, were in McDonalds in Toronto, Canada, and were amused to see a copy of the book protruding from a customer's pocket!

The Head Librarian in Glasgow read it and arranged for copies to be placed in the Mitchell Library, and every public library in Glasgow. A local librarian told me recently that copies of the book were being stolen from the libraries. This may be an inadvertent form of flattery An author should not be pleased that instead of buying their own copy, people are passing the book around relatives, or as someone told me recently, around the fellow-residents of a close in Drumchapel. At least the author's epitaph is coming true -'I always hoped that when I were dead, though my sins were as scarlet, my books were read.' I think there is some sales evidence to show that there was a revival of interest in the book on the back of the publication of Revival Man - the Jock Troup Story which I wrote in 2002.

I give humble thanks to God that the book has been a blessing and an encouragement to some to come to faith in Christ, and to their 'first love' of Him.

I no longer live in Inverness, nor have the privilege of watching Inverness Caledonian Thistle, although I travelled with some fans to Glasgow, and was there on the night when they put the mighty Glasgow Celtic out of the Scottish Cup.

We have some good friends in Drumchapel, Glasgow, but did not settle there. We live now in retirement at the foot of the Campsie Fells, near our family and handy for preaching appointments all over the place, from Prestwick to Peterhead, from Partick to Pittenweem, from Cumbernauld to Carlisle, and from Johnstone to Jersey. In closing, I would like to express thanks to Christian Focus for this third reprint, which I pray may continue to be a blessing to all who read it.

George Mitchell.   March 2003

POSTSCRIPT 2, for 5th reprint

A good number of people keep asking to buy copies of 'Comfy Glasgow'. I have edited it, extended it and illustrated it, and hope that it will be well received. I have bought a publisher's licence, and the fifth reprint goes out with the approval of Christian Focus, and the help of Kenwil Print and Design, to whom I am deeply grateful.

I have noticed that since I have retired, Terry Butcher has taken over as Manager of Caley Thistle, and my earlier comments have been superseded since their ground has now become a 'fortress' under his leadership, feared by any visiting teams.

I will take space to include two stories concerning the book, by way of update.

A Baptist minister, who is a school chaplain, visited his school, and found a Primary Seven class using the book as a reading book! When he told the teacher that he knew the author, they organised a 'meet the author' session where I went along to answer the children's (should we be calling them 'students' now?) questions. The head teacher was there, bought the book, contacted the Pastor, and became a Christian...I hope I don't go to jail for this...

The second story arose through a conversation with a senior Army chaplain, who told me there were several copies of 'Comfy Glasgow' in the Army base in Helmand Province, Afghanistan. He said that the Jocks were always reading it, and that the problem was (the same as with Glasgow Public Libraries) to prevent them stealing it. He told me more than twenty of his unit had been killed and over a hundred wounded, and that this would probably be the only Christian book that many of them would read.

The story continues...July 2011